I0366065

KUNG FU
SELF-DEFENSE
FIGHT BACK

— REVISED EDITION —

by Eric Lee

EMPIRE BOOK/AWP LLC
Los Angeles, CA.

Disclaimer

Please note that the author and publisher of this book are NOT RESPONSIBLE in any manner whatsoever for any injury that may result from practicing the techniques and/or following the instructions given within. Since the physical activities described herein may be too strenuous in nature for some readers to engage in safely, it is essential that a physician be consulted prior to training.

Revised Edition published in 2021 by AWP LLC/Empire Books. Copyright (c) 2021 by Eric Lee and AWP LLC/Empire Books.

All rights reserved. No part of this publication may be reproduced or utilized in any form or by any means, electronic or mechanical, including photo- copying, recording, or by any information storage and retrieval system, without prior written permission from AWP LLC/Empire Books.

Revised edition Library of Congress Catalog Number:

ISBN-13: 978-1-949753-80-6

21 20 19 18 17 16 15 14 13 12

Library of Congress Cataloging-in-Publication Data

Kung Fu Fight Back Self- Defense by Eric Lee -- ed. p. cm.

ISBN 978-1-949753-80-6 (pbk. : alk. paper) 1. Martial arts-- philosophy. 3. Large type books. I. Title. GV1114.3.F715 20713261.815'3--dc22

20063331981

Printed in the United States of America.

KUNG FU
SELF-DEFENSE
FIGHT BACK

— REVISED EDITION —

ACKNOWLEDGEMENTS

I would like to thank the following people for their efforts and assistance in preparing this book: my students and friends who posed for the photos, Julio Hernandez, Mark Vorbau, Karen Shepard, Joe Stobbs and Gary Forbach. I would also like to thank my associates at Unique Publications: publisher, Curtis Wong; photographers, Ed Ikuta and David King; layout and design, Jeff Dungfelder; editors, Bob Mendel, Sandra Segal and Daniel M. Furuya.

DEDICATION

I would like to dedicate this book to my teachers in the martial arts with special thanks to Sifu Al Dacascos.

TABLE OF CONTENTS

INTRODUCTION
What Would You Do If ? 12
The Purpose of This Book 24
The Five Principles of Self-Defense 26
Summary 27

CHAPTER ONE
A Look at Violence and Some Solutions 30
Tactics Against Rape 32
Techniques Against Rape 33
Summary 45

CHAPTER TWO
Personal Security and Natural Weapons 48
Conflicts You Can Prevent 49
Questions and Answers About Safety 50
Fighting Back 52
Pressure Point Targets 56
Simple Attacks to Vulnerable Area 57
Built-in Weapons 58
The Voice 59

CHAPTER THREE
Tactics Against Locks, Holds and Chokes 42
Summary 125

CHAPTER FOUR
Situational Self-Defense 128
Summary 144

CHAPTER FIVE
Special Problems 146
Danger of Weapons and Multiple Attackers 174
Summary 191

CHAPTER SIX
Body Toning Techniques 194
Three Basic Warmup Exercises 196
Stretching Exercises 197
Summary 203

CHAPTER SEVEN
Mental Preparation and Training 206
Concentration Exercises 207
Awareness and Attitude 209

CHAPTER EIGHT
How to Choose A Self-Defense School 214
Do's and Don'ts 215
General Review Quiz 216
Review Quiz Answers 218
Conclusions 219
Eric Lee: King of Kata 220
Interview - Eric Lee: The King of Forms 223

INTRODUCTION

What would you do if . . .

You are sitting alone on a bench one evening and a stranger approaches, sits down and begins putting his arm around you?

You are at your car, about to unlock it, and a man approaches you from behind in an aggressive way and grabs your shoulder?

You have just left your bank with some money and as you turn the corner, a man steps into your path, holds a knife in front of you and then starts to attack you with it?

The first thing to do is not to panic. This will only reduce your chances of taking the right course of action. Second, evaluate the situation. If you can talk your way out of it, that's better than fighting and taking a chance of being injured.

In situation number one, the woman may be able to reason with the aggressor. In situation number two, the man has already become physical and threatening. In situation number three, it is important to determine whether the robber simply is using the knife as a threat in order to take the money, or whether he is ready to attack. If he is going to attack you, there is no choice, you must defend yourself against physical harm.

The purpose of this book is to teach the reader to identify basic situations of danger and take the most reasonable and appropriate course of action. This book does not teach you to "fight": it teaches you how to maintain your own personal safety in the simplest and most practical way.

The actions taken by the people shown in the photos are not only just simple and effective techniques but demonstrate some important principles that you can utilize in your own personal self-defense. Situations, like these, arise in real life constantly but never follow a predictable pattern. You must learn effective methods to deal with violence and preventative measures, which are equally important, that will help you reduce your chances of becoming a "victim."

The assailant approaches the woman sitting on a bench and opens a conversation in an aggressive and threatening way. She tries to ignore his advances.

He sits down, very close to her and begins to make physical advances. Since he initiated physical contact by putting his arm around her, she is justified in responding to this threat.

The woman quickly notes the exposed area of his face and body close to her and launches an elbow strike to the head.

The strike connects, driving the assailant's head and neck back sharply and causing severe pain to the nose and mouth area. Before he can recover, she turns and grabs his hair at the front and back of the head.

Standing and moving her weight to the right foot, she brings his head down quickly to meet her left knee, which is brought up in a short, sharp kick. The movement bringing the attacker's head toward the oncoming kick provides maximum impact.

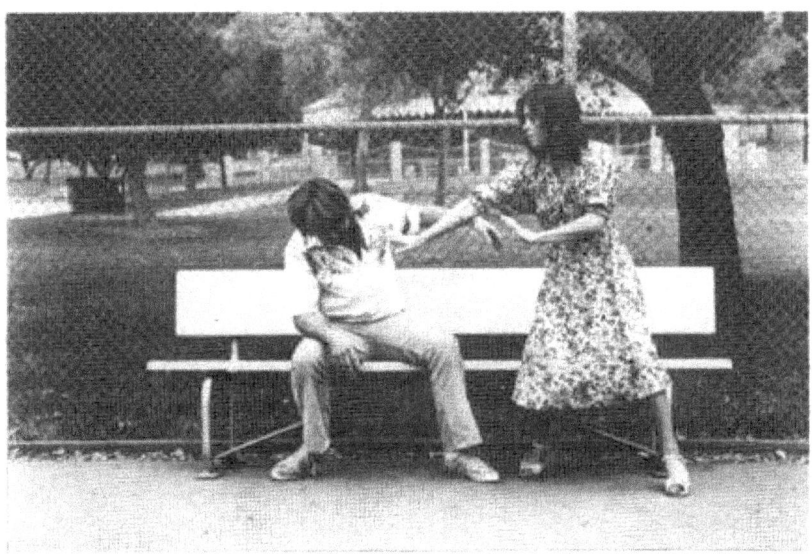

Taking advantage of his shock and injury, the woman makes good her escape.

The principle involved in this situation is the fact that the victim is not really at a disadvantage. She has a weapon, if she recognizes the fact, in her keys. She strikes to an area where this kind of weapon will do serious and immediate damage. The attacker is unlikely to be able to recover at all, much less to recover quickly, and she will be able to get away safely. Note that a strike to the chest, or arm, or some fairly hard part of the body would not provide anywhere near as much of a chance of success with this kind of short weapon.

The attacker approaches his intended victim as she prepares to get into her car. He may have seen her jogging and followed her, planning his rape.

The assailant reaches out and grasps the arm of the victim, and at this point she decides that his physical attack calls for self-defense. Note that she turns toward the attacker, rather than trying to pull away, since he is stronger and already close to her.

The victim grasps her car keys firmly, the door or ignition key held like a small weapon.

She strikes directly to a vulnerable area, the attacker's eyes, causing intense pain and temporary blindness. She will either run for help if someone is within sight, or drive away before he can recover.

The attacker has threatened Eric with a knife. As the victim Eric (you) must decide whether to go along with the assailant by agreeing to his demands, in the case of robbery, or whether he intends to use the knife. In this case, the assailant is advancing with the weapon and Eric decides to act.

Eric steps forward with the right foot and strikes toward the eyes with his right hand while grasping the wrist of the assailant's knife hand with his left hand. The movement must be made simultaneously, so that the hand that strikes toward the eyes covers the move to grab the wrist.

Eric drops the right hand and also secures the knife hand by gripping it and begins to maneuver this hand. Because this hand holds a sharp weapon, both the victim and the assailant will concentrate on it rather than using other strikes or moves. If the hand did not hold a knife, Eric would not grab it with both his hands, leaving the assailant one free hand to attack with.

Eric moves the knife hand in a natural arch up and in. This brings the knife blade across the face of the attacker. He will either be cut seriously or be forced to pull his head and face back quickly, leaving him off-balance and on the defensive.

Having gained control and leverage, Eric continues the movement in the same arch now bending the arm out and back in a painful control hold. At the same time, he prepares for a full take down by raising his front leg to change position. He is able to cross in front of the attacker because he is on balance and in control, and he is moving in one direction with his entire body.

Eric is now in a low stance with his weight centered. The attacker is being forced back over Eric's leg, which is used to trip him. Note how Eric has kept his own elbows in tight and close to his chest, maximizing his leverage. The attacker must fall.

The conclusion of the technique finds the attacker down and Eric maintaining a control lock on the weapon hand. Practice is required to make sure that the technique is executed smoothly and with the proper foot work. Do not practice with a real knife—substitute a stick or rubber knife.

The Purpose Of This Book

The purpose of this book is not to make you into a great streetfighter. It is to help you minimize your chances of becoming a victim. In order to accomplish this, there are necessary facts and concepts you must know, the proper attitude to take in an emergency, techniques that you should practice, and above all, the cultivation of your mental awareness and common sense. It just might save your life one day.

This book is for everyone from the complete novice to the practicing martial artist. The techniques that are shown are offered in a basic and simple style with more advanced alternatives in some cases. The advanced forms of technique are for martial artists who have developed a certain amount of physical control and mental awareness and now want to build a sense of how they can apply what they know to self-defense situations on the street.

This book is also designed to help you gain a sense of proportion in situations involving stress or conflict so that you can take the right course of action, whether that course is talking, running or resisting.

First, when careful preventive measures are taken in your daily life you can immediately reduce the chances that you will become a victim or a part of a situation that results in violence. On the other hand, no one can insure that you will not be accosted by an assailant at some time. This is why preparation is necessary.

By taking steps to prepare yourself, you can lower your anxiety level about going out in public or being safe in your own neighborhood or home. Many people really allow themselves to be victimized because they have not been trained or educated to cope with an emergency. This book will cover a wide range of preparatory measures of all kinds.

The purpose of this book is to show you practical self-defense techniques and preventive measures. The techniques are practical in two ways: 1) they really work, and 2) you can master them if you are willing to practice them.

Many of the preventive measures are tips that can help you by simply knowing what to do. For example, did you know that if you are being threatened by someone outside it is better to yell, "Fire" than to shout, "Help." Why? When you call for help, many people are afraid to get involved or believe it is a family or personal argument. When you shout "Fire," everyone wants to know where it is and what is going on. This could thwart and frighten an attacker away before he has a chance to injure you.

If you use this book as a basis for practice, you cannot only gain confidence and understand the mind of the attacker but also understand yourself better as well. You can learn the best way to deal with emergencies concerning yourself, your spouse and your family. As you progress, you will start to feel stronger, healthier and have better resistance to illness.

Many techniques shown in this book are depicted in the environment where they would normally take place. This is done as a reminder that where, and how, a problem takes place can dictate the course of action you should take. There is no predictable or patterned way to handle violence but if you develop a better awareness of your surroundings you can function more effectively.

After practicing the techniques in your home for a period of time, you should also practice them outside in various locations with a partner, taking turns simulating an attack. This can help you to make sure you can apply the technique under stress or utilize something in the environment as an aid to resisting the assailant.

These are things you should know and remember that can give you an advantage in dealing with violence. This book will show you that there are:

*built-in weapons you can use.

*common objects that are always with you that can be turned to weapons.

*simple tricks to help you avoid being victimized.

*vulnerable areas you can strike even if the attacker is stronger than you.

*factors that make rape a special situation with special solutions.

*exercises that help you gain power, flexibility and coordination.

*mental factors like attitude and concentration which are equally as important as physical ability and strength.

The Five Principles of Self Defense

To make sure that you don't become the victim of violence you must be prepared to defend yourself fully—with an all-out counterattack. There are some principles that apply to a successful effort at resisting violence. The five elements of your self-defense technique should be:

1) It should be *simple:* complex or elaborate techniques can fail through lack of proper execution or too much time required to do them.

2) It should be a *surprise:* a good technique should catch your assailant unaware or unprepared, otherwise he may forestall it.

3) *Speed* is essential: the attacker is not going to cooperate with your technique or wait for it. Speed also increases power.

4) *Impact* is vital: this means the technique should hurt or disable the assailant. If it does not, he will be angered and make it worse for you.

5) You must *follow-up*: the follow-up can be a second strike, or series of strikes, or running away while the attacker is stunned or in severe pain. In any case, you must free yourself from the situation and the role of being the victim.

To repeat the five elements of successful response to violence: Simplicity; Surprise; Speed; Impact; and Follow-up. These elements will become clearer as you familiarize yourself with the techniques. In the meantime, regular and continued practice will help you develop the ability to defend yourself successfully.

Summary

The major objectives of this book include the following:

1) To teach the right attitude, behavior and procedure in minimizing the possibility that you will become a victim.

2) To teach self-defense techniques that will protect your physical and mental well-being.

3) To relieve anxiety or fear of violence in daily living.

4) To prevent you being victimized because you have not been educated or prepared to cope with an emergency situation involving a threat or assault.

CHAPTER ONE

A Look At Violence And Some Solutions

A Look at Violence

We know that many people are seriously concerned with what appears to be a major upswing in violence occurring in the major cities of the United States. One set of recent statistics based on an FBI survey shows the following:

Every three seconds a crime takes place.
Every twenty-seven minutes a murder takes place.
Every one and a half minutes a robbery takes place.
Every minute an aggravated assault takes place.
Every three minutes a crime involving property takes place.

Another recent survey concluded that throughout the US, one out of every three persons would be touched by crime. The police are the first to admit that they don't have the manpower or resources to provide adequate protection for us all. It is up to us to take care of ourselves. But there is not enough information generally available about how to best take care of our property and our lives through preventive measures and common sense. We, however, can begin to look at the basic measures for self-protection here.

Self-defense instruction is based on the assumption that escape from danger or avoiding it is our first and most effective choice of action. Successful resistance to attack does not mean winning a fight—it means escaping bodily harm or injury. Some people who learn self-defense overestimate their own abilities and may take a greater risk than they can handle. They will probably suffer for this.

Unless you learn to do the right thing in an emergency, you may do the wrong thing and suffer the consequences. Panic blocks positive action but someone who is prepared for an emergency is less likely to panic. Self-defense does not mean you are committed to fight. Learning a sound self-defense method can prevent reckless behavior. To understand what takes place in a conflict, we should try to see what goes on in the mind of the attacker. People who prey on others are, at least in one sense, mentally ill. This doesn't excuse their behavior but it tells us that they must be treated with caution. Maintaining your own self-control is the beginning. There is nothing wrong with turning away from a crazed individual or a childish challenge to fight.

You may be able to calm someone who is upset or angry but be careful. Try to analyze the person's body language and determine what they are likely to do. If the attacker has a weapon, you must decide if he intends to use it right away or if he uses it as a threat to rob you. When an armed assailant holds a knife or a gun on you and says,"give me your money," the best thing to do is give it to him promptly. Your life and health is worth more than a few dollars. Police advise that even if you carry a can of mace or a weapon, but the time you get it out, you may be wounded or worse.

Do not negotiate for your belongings or delay the criminal. He is already nervous and delay will only frustrate and anger him. If you are in an isolated area, do not scream. If your wallet or money is tucked away, do not move suddenly for it but assure the criminal that you are only getting it from that pocket. Above all, do not force someone to use his weapon on you.

If, on the other hand, the person is already undertaking an attack on you, whether with a knife or not, you really have no choice. You must try to save your own life. If someone in your immediate area looks suspicious, try to locate some kind of weapon to use, like your keys, mace, or a comb. Be prepared, rather than sorry.

Research shows that in forty percent of personal assault, the victim was on the ground before he or she could react. If you carry a weapon, like mace, it must be where you can get it quickly. The best place to carry the small mace canisters is on your key chain. If it is buried in your purse, or in a glove compartment, you may never have the chance to get it out. Many people are also bullied with their own weapons, so if you decide to use one, do not hesitate.

If your attacker has a knife and you are sure you can outrun them, flee for safety. If not, try to assess whether or not the knife is used just as a threat to rob you, or whether the attacker is planning to actually use the weapon.

Do not let the attacker see you as a passive, helpless victim. Studies show that body language and behavior is used by attackers when making a choice of their victims. Try to be confident, alert and decisive in your actions and manner. If an assailant stops you, never plead for mercy. This tells the assailant that you are helpless, frightened and incapable of taking action. This encourages the attacker and gives him confidence. Instead, behave as though you are angry but under control.

Tactics Against Rape

Rape is a special problem in many ways. Very often, unlike other types of assault, the criminal plans his crime over a period of time. Some forty percent of the rapes that occur take place in the victim's own home. Proper personal security and home security could eliminate this opportunity for the rapist. Another forty percent of rapes occur in the street. Twenty percent happen by chance. Here again, caution in preventive measures can reduce the chance of this happening. Statistics also show that sixty percent of the rapists use force to get their way and of those who use force, ninety-three percent continue to use force throughout the attack.

The next factor concerning rape is that the rapist must come very close to the victim and this presents, at least, some opportunity for resistance. Police recommend talking to the rapist, primarily as a means of distracting him while you look for an opening to strike. Since, on the average, men are stronger than women and are used to fighting, the element of surprise is vital.

"Don't hurt me, I'll give you anything you want..." is one way to begin. As the rapist relaxes, keep talking, say anything but maintain eye contact and try to force him to get involved in the conversation. As he gets in close, suddenly strike hard and fast with the knee to a groin and a jab into the eyes and then run. Scream "fire" as you run. He should be in extreme pain and unable to pursue you and perhaps unable to see for a moment or two.

Some women have been successful by telling the rapist that they have venereal disease, were menstruating or were pregnant. Tears are a bad idea, since they bring out the sadist in the attacker and rape is more of a crime of violence than of sex. If someone is following you and you suspect rape, you can pretend being strange or mentally disturbed. Throw him off his plan. The best policy of all is avoidance of those places or situations where a rapist can approach you.

Above all, do not hitchhike, particularly in a bikini which is an invitation for rape or at best a very unpleasant scene. Rape from hitchhiking occurs more than any other kind of assault.

Techniques Against Rape

There are some techniques that can be applied to the situation in which the rapist has already gotten his victim to the ground. Since this can happen very quickly in many cases, it is important to practice the techniques demonstrated here.

Perhaps the most important general rule to remember is not to get into a wrestling match with the rapist. Since, on the average, the male is stronger and has a superior position established, this wastes your strength and even encourages the rapist to increase his violence. Instead, conserve your strength, choose a target and strike suddenly. Escape is your most important consideration.

This technique illustrates several principles recommended in defense against rape. The first is that the woman chose not to struggle and wrestle with the rapist since she is at the disadvantage from the first. Second, she delivered a quick and surprise strike to a very vulnerable area. Her one advantage lay in the fact that the assailant did not have a gun or knife with which to threaten her and that, as in all cases of rape, he had to come in close to her which would sooner or later provide an opening for a counterattack.

Finally, she did not waste time in getting away once she had turned the tables on the attacker.

Alone in the park, a woman is accosted by a male assailant. Before she can think of escape, he is upon her.

He grabs her and pushes her to the ground immediately, and she recognizes that he plans to rape her.

As she falls, she has instinctively begun to use the best weapon available at the moment, cocking her knee.

Using the ground for leverage, she drives her knee into the assailant's exposed groin area, causing sharp and sudden pain.

As the assailant doubles over in pain, losing his balance, the woman takes advantage of the situation to get away quickly and run for help.

The victim has been caught like many others in rape cases, and finds herself on the ground before she knew what happened. She also has her hands and arms pinned down in what seems to be a very vulnerable position. The use of a sudden movement; however, is enough to move the assailant and shift his balance so that his leverage is no longer effective. This alone would not be sufficient to help her and it is important that he is not allowed a moment to compensate for this. She must strike to the groin at the same time that she distracts him.

Her arms are pinned back on the ground, but the assailant must straddle her to do this.

The victim makes a strong and sudden movement to shoot her arms back and up, causing the attacker to lose his center of balance slightly and to distract him as well. At the same time, she prepares to knee him in the groin area which is exposed in this position.

As she knees the assailant, the victim rolls him to one side strongly taking advantage of his relaxing his grip in the midst of the unexpected pain.

As he rolls off, she quickly gets up and runs away from him. She runs for safety.

In this case, the position of the rapist is too far forward to allow the victim to use her legs to any advantage. But the principle illustrated here is that there is always a vulnerable target and an available weapon. Surprise and a sudden strike are necessary and effective moves.

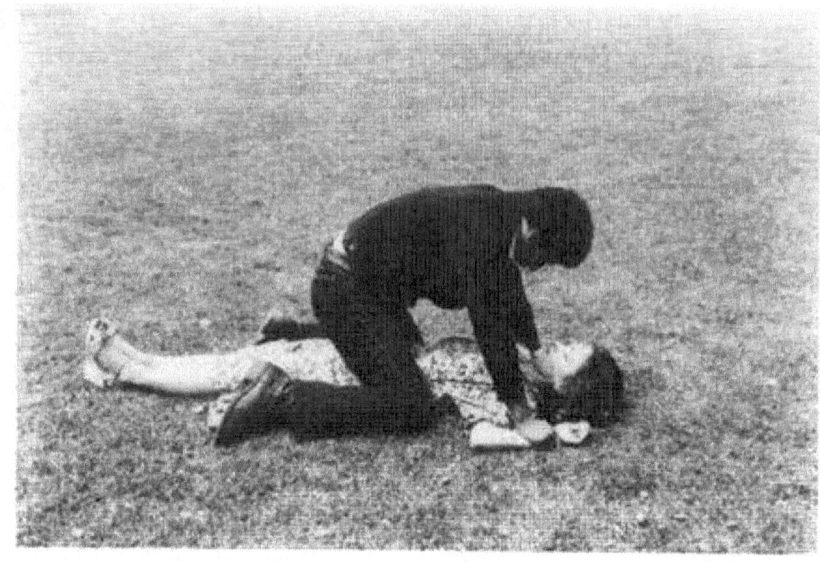

The woman may sense that the man is crouched over her hips where she cannot easily reach him with a knee to the groin, because he is so far forward.

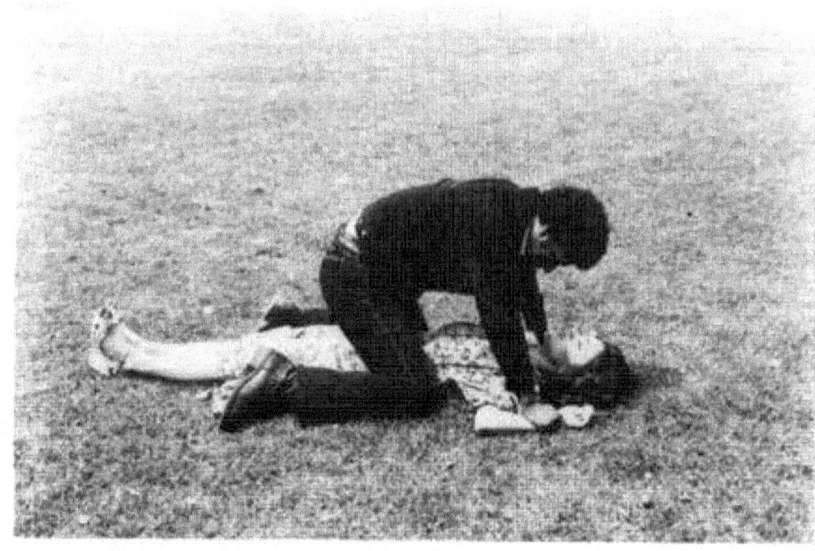

But as he moves closer to her face she strikes upward with her head smashing her forehead into his nose causing a sudden and intense pain.

She follows up by rolling the rapist off as she did in the preceeding technique.

In this case, the victim is able to take advantage of the second stage in a rape attack in which the assailant is attempting to tear away her clothing. To do so, he must use his hands and this presents the victim with a real opportunity. She strikes to the most vulnerable spot in the body available, the eyes. But temporarily blinding or hurting the assailant is not enough. She must use the strike to free herself from danger, so she combines the strike with a twisting movement that will throw the rapist off balance and allow her to get up and get away.

The rapist has his victim on the ground and is preparing to rip her dress. Although the assailant has the superior position, the victim's hands are left free by his move to rip open the dress.

The victim grabs the hair and ears of the attacker with both hands and twists it suddenly to the side, wrenching his neck and digging her thumbs into his eyes, causing extreme pain.

She continues by pulling his face back, gathering strength and rolling to one side quickly while shoving his face with her hands and his body with her legs, throwing him off.

Before he can recover, she gets up and runs to safety.

Summary

Self-defense is based on the idea that our major goal is to avoid danger and injury. This is not the same thing as winning a fight. Panic or fear blocks positive action and can result in taking the wrong course of action. Try to remain calm in an emergency.

If you can negotiate with a criminal, do so. If robbery is the attacker's motive, give him what he wants. If there is a direct threat of violence, you have no real choice except to defend yourself from physical danger or injury.

Weapons may tip the balance in your favor but they can also be turned against you. To be effective, any weapon must be where it can be reached very quickly in an emergency and used effectively.

Rape is a unique situation because the rapist often plans his crime. Many women are attacked and forced to the ground before they know what has happened. Avoid situations like hitchhiking if you are a woman. Do not wrestle with the rapist but seek an opportunity to surprise him with a sudden, lethal strike. Use your voice if people are nearby.

CHAPTER TWO

Personal Security & Natural Weapons

Personal Security

There are many common sense preventive measures you can take to reduce the chance of attack.

THE TELEPHONE

If you get a phone call from a stranger do not let him know that you are going out or whether or not you are alone. This might present the opportunity he has been looking for to break into your home or to attack you.

Don't allow strangers to use your phone. If they need emergency aid, make the necessary phone call for them while they wait outside.

Have emergency numbers such as police, fire, doctor taped to the phone for quick reference.

THE CAR

Do not give rides to hitchhikers. Park in well-lit areas at night and avoid darkened or lonely parking lots. Make sure your car, including the back seat is empty before you get into it. Never leave your car unlocked when you park it. When you get in, lock all the doors immediately. If someone appoaches or threatens you, use the car horn to attract attention. If the car is disabled, raise the hood and then sit in the car with the doors locked until the police arrive. Take brighter, main roads to your destination when driving at night. Keep your car in tune with enough gas, oil and water when you commute or drive at night.

WALKING ALONE

If you jog or run, avoid doing it late at night or in dark, deserted places. Take a dog with you if possible or carry a small mace cylinder. Make sure you know how to use the mace properly.

If you work late, make sure a security guard or fellow employee knows you are there and can accompany you to your car. Try not to be alone.

IN YOUR HOME

Try not to let casual strangers know whether or not you live alone. Put initials and last name only on the mailbox. Don't leave duplicate door keys hidden outside. Do not use an apartment laundry room alone at night and be careful of elevators at odd hours.

When a repairman arrives that you don't know, ask him to furnish his identification or make a call to his employer to verify the call. If he is legitimate, he will understand your precautions. Use a deadbolt lock and a wide-angle peephole on your door. Do not open the door to strangers until you are sure of their business. If you return home and someone is there, do not enter but get aid from a neighbor or, preferably, the police. A startled burglar may shoot or injure you.

Conflicts You Can Prevent

One type of danger is the situation in which a criminal is bent on rape or robbery and you get in the way. The other kind of conflict is the one in which you play a part by contributing to the tension or violence. This occurs when you get into arguments or disputes through pride or frustration leading to violence. We all have to remember that our life and wellbeing are our greatest possession and they should not be endangered or taken lightly. When we are sufficiently angered or frustrated by someone we can often gamble our own safety because of ego and its involvement at the moment. This kind of poor self-control could cost you life or limb.

Even if you win the immediate conflict that results, there can be a legal or physical retaliation that follows. It isn't unusual for someone to lose a fight, go and get some friends and return to take revenge. Using your common sense means that we should take all the necessary means available to us to avoid a conflict and leave the situation as friends instead of enemies. It is said that a boy becomes a man when he walks around a puddle instead of through it.

Legally, you are also obligated to avoid violence and if you don't have a chance to call the police for help, you will have to prove that you had no alternative to self-defense. In this case, it means that your actions were self-protective and not retaliatory. You must show that you did not go beyond what was necessary for your own self-defense and personal safety.

On the other hand, you are not required to leave the vicinity in which you work or live to avoid difficulty with a criminal. But this is still the most intelligent thing to do if you are not able to remain emotionally uninvolved when you are attacked. However, your well-being is not dependent on the whim of an attacker and you are allowed to protect yourself against immoral and illegal attack. Many times you may be able to deliver your own crippling strike before the assailant makes an attempt on you. By all means, attack first rather than take a chance on being killed or crippled in such a situation.

Questions & Answers About Safety

Here are some typical questions that relate to the issue of self-defense and violence.

Will I become a dangerous person through studying self-defense?

You are only as dangerous as your mind. Your mind controls your physical actions. You want to do things because your mind tells you to do them. If you want to learn self-defense it is because you want to protect yourself from harm and rightfully so. This is why it is self-defense, not self-offense.

How do I learn to control myself in emergencies?

The first thing you learn is not to over-react when something happens suddenly. When you over-react, it means that you lose your own center of balance momentarily. By this, mental and emotional balance is defined. You learn to remain calm at all times and helping you to make more sense of many kinds of situations.

To cultivate this kind of control, the practice of meditation is helpful. This is one reason that meditation techniques have often been associated with martial arts training in the past and today as well. Beyond helping you to calm yourself mentally, meditation helps release physical stress and tension. It also helps increase your energy and makes your thinking clearer.

There are many places where you can practice mediation such as in a group or class in addition to practicing at home. Yoga, tai chi chuan, kung fu, karate and other martial arts schools often include meditation in their training. In the meantime, there are some basic meditation exercises recommended in this book to develop this dimension of your training. Your mind plays an equally important part in your practice for self-defense as your body. In many ways, it is the starting point.

What is the best way to avoid a fight?

Try to talk your way out of it. This requires being calm and clear. Sometimes it can be advisable to strike first and disable your assailant. In case of a threat to your health or safety, anything goes. There are no rules.

Where do most robberies take place?

Most robberies take place in crowded, public places like bus stations or street corners, train and air terminals . . . not just in so-called "bad" neighborhoods.

What attracts the robber?

An exposed wallet or money, jewelry or a purse or other signs that you have something of value may attract a robber to you.

How can you deal with an unavoidable fight with two assailants?

Pick the larger of the two or the obvious leader and kick or strike him suddenly with speed and full force. Try to move to one side of him so that he becomes a shield between you and the other assailant. You should try to maneuver so that you are usually fighting only one of the two at any one time rather than trying to deal with two attackers simultaneously.

What can you do in a case of attempted rape?

If you are outside, scream "FIRE" and run for safety if at all possible. If there is no available escape, try a sudden surprise attack to a vital area, such as the rapist's groin, throat or eyes. Then run.

What is the value of a gun for self-defense?

Any weapon, including a gun, is only good for protection if it is readily available when you need it. For example, you may not have time to get the gun or get a can of mace from your purse in a sudden and critical emergency. A gun also means that you must be mentally and emotionally mature enough to have self-control at all times. Statistics show that guns injure or kill spouses and family members more often than criminals.

Why is there so much gun violence?

There are a variety of reasons. The widespread use of drugs contributes to crime and violence. In addition to criminal use, in many cases, a gun user is involved in a business dispute, or an emotional situation concerning a personal relationship . . . between parents and children, lovers, jilted lovers, or cases where alcohol adds to jealousy and leads to anger and rage.

What about a dog for protection?

The police feel that a dog who barks at intruders is one of the better deterrents to robbery in the home. But in terms of personal defense, a dog is an unreliable method unless it is thoroughly trained to protect you.

What do you do if someone is in your home and their actions begin to make you uncomfortable?

Ask them to leave immediately. If they refuse, leave yourself and seek outside help by phoning the police or a neighbor.

In an argument, what helps prevent violence?

Pursuing legal action, seeking professional counselling or therapy or just leaving the situation until it can be resolved at another time. The options mentioned above require professional help and they are worthwhile if they prevent physical harm and determine the difference between life or death.

What do you do if you are threatened by a dog?

Although it sounds unusual, it is not unlikely that you will happen upon a hostile dog somewhere along the line. People who walk or jog regularly are often confronted by a dog who resents the invasion of its territory. What should you do?

Try to walk away slowly in another direction and find a new route to where you want to go. If the dog pursues you and you have the time, wrap a jacket around one arm and let him grab at that, rather than let him get to your hand or throat. As he grabs the wrapped arm, you can strike him on the top of the nose area. If that is difficult, try to kick up under his throat.

If you are bitten, get a medical examination for rabies and report the incident to the police so the dog can be checked as well. Do not try to intimidate the dog, throw something at him, or shout since this is likely to aggravate the situation.

Fighting Back

If you are faced with an emergency, you have more weapons at your disposal than you may have ever thought about. They are common objects that you carry with you everyday ... like a pen, pencil, spray can, hairbrush, or even the handy credit card.

They become weapons if they are used correctly and with the element of surprise. They can cause a great deal of damage, severe pain, and allow you to escape without the attacker touching you.

The credit card is hard plastic and this, together with its sharp edge, makes it an effective weapon. Hold it firmly between your fingers and use it to cut across the attacker's eyes, as shown. This will temporarily blind him and you can get away or get help.

Your key ring with its sharp, pointed, pressed metal keys is an obvious weapon. Hold the key ring with the key points protruding from your hand. Rake your hand across the attacker's face, and get away while he is reacting to the pain.

The common hairbrush, which you may have at hand, in a purse, or any other hard plastic object like it, also becomes a weapon. Grasp it firmly and, as the attacker grabs for you, bring it up in a sudden thrust to a vulnerable spot like the throat.

The can of hairspray, also found in the home, or a can of spray paint, air deodorant, or bug killer, all of which are common to the home or office, is also a weapon. Use it to spray into the eyes of the attacker and escape while he remains blinded.

These are just several of a wide range of things that can be easily turned into weapons. A purse, a shoe, any pointed object, any cutting edge, any solid object that is handy and can be used quickly and easily. Use what is at hand to turn the tables on the attacker.

There are certain highly vulnerable spots on the body, sometimes called pressure points where severe damage can be done even without great physical strength. They should be among your first choice of targets if your life or health are threatened and in danger. Quick use of these vulnerable points may save you from serious injury in a conflict.

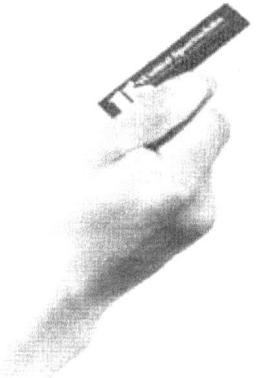

Holding a credit card as a weapon.

Striking attacker's eyes with a credit card.

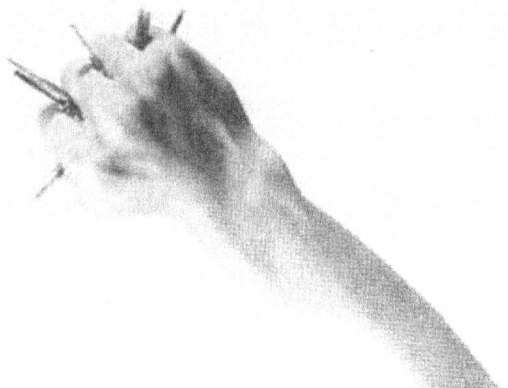

Holding keys as a weapon.

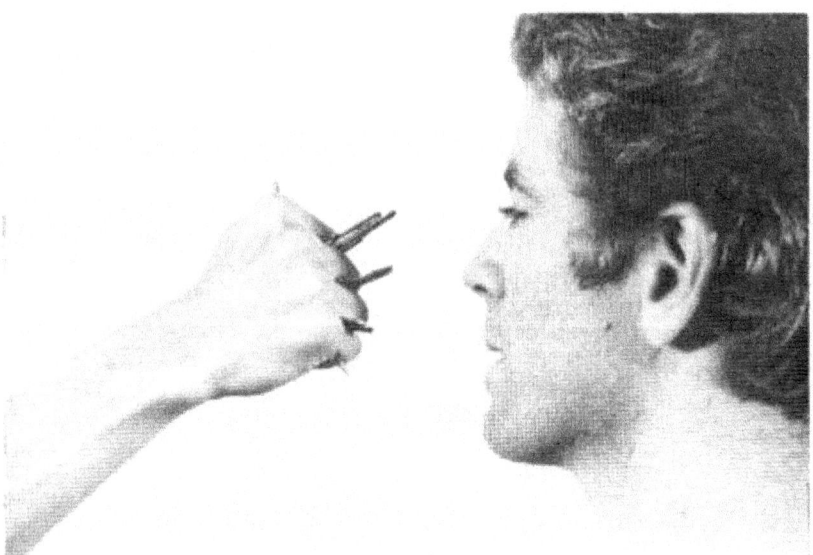

Using the keys against the attacker's face.

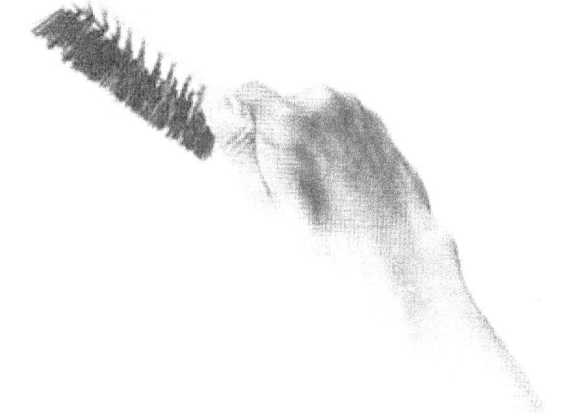

Holding a hair brush as a weapon.

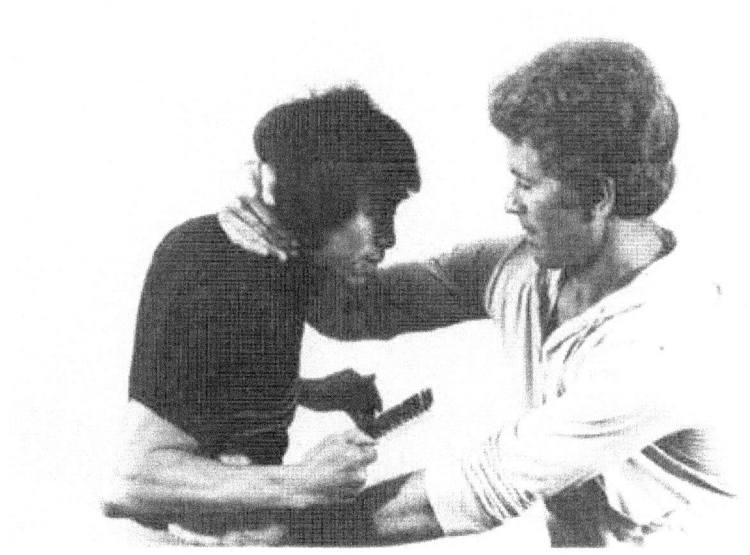

Using the hair brush against the attacker.

Pressure Point Targets

The best pressure points available for attack include the following:
1) The area just below the ears.
2) The temple.
3) The soft area behind the collarbone.
4) The Adam's apple.
5) The base of the neck.

You must be ready to strike to these points in case of serious danger to your safety but a moving attacker can be hard to strike. Use surprise to enhance your chance of success. There are some effective ways to make your strike to these targets most effective and they include the following:
1) Push your thumb into the space below the ear.
2) Use your knuckles to strike the temple.
3) Push your hand under the collarbone.
4) Push your thumbs into the Adam's apple.
5) Strike the base of the neck or throat.

Simple Attacks To Vulnerable Areas

There are some other ways to deter or stop the attack if someone is threatening you. They do not require a great deal of practice just the presence of mind. Anyone, even physically weak people, can make this kind of method work against a larger or stronger person because the target area is so vulnerable to injury.

These simple methods include the following:
1) Pull on the hair at the back of the head.
2) Pull on the long sideburns.
3) Push the thumbs into the eyesockets.
4) Drive the heel of the palm into the under part of the nose and force up and back.
5) Use the knuckles to strike Adam's apple area.
6) Use the palm heel to drive up under the chin.
7) Use a chopping motion to the throat.

These strikes will be shown in action in following chapters, so that you can see how they work under attack. They are extremely effective and, when practicing them, contact should not be made to these areas for safety's sake. Use them only when you are in imminent danger of harm or injury or where there is a serious threat to your life. These are real self-defense techniques and not exercises or sports playing.

Built-In Weapons

There are a number of parts on your own body that work as built-in weapons if they are used correctly. Your fist is not the only way to inflict damage. Try to use the best weapons available at any given time. Your other weapons include:

1) The fingernails for raking and clawing.
2) The heel of foot for stomping and kicking.
3) The knee for short close-in kicks.
4) The elbow for close-in strikes.
5) The thumbs for gouging.
6) The heel of the hand for striking.
7) The feet for kicking and tripping.
8) The head for butting.
9) The teeth for biting.
10) The fingers for jabbing.

There are other general body areas that are particularly vulnerable to attack, which are well-known to most people. These include the groin, solar plexus, shins and feet. One or more of these areas is usually exposed to attack when you are in the grip of an attacker.

Often, there is a natural link between certain built-in weapons you have and a vulnerable target area on your attacker. The two just naturally go together. Among these are the following:

Elbow to the solar plexus. This is even more accessible when the attacker grabs you from behind.

Knee to the groin which is useful when the attacker pulls you in close to him.

Kick to the shins which works as the attacker steps in to threaten you.

Heel stomp to the foot which can be done when you are being held from behind or when your hands are restrained by the attacker.

In the techniques demonstrated in the following chapters, you will see these methods used over and over because they do not depend on overpowering your attacker, great speed, or unusual ability. They can work for you. The key to using them is to remain calm and locate the opening available to you in whatever situation you are in.

The Voice

One of the built-in weapons you are likely to overlook is your own voice. It can be used both defensively and offensively. Do not hesitate to scream at the top of your lungs for help before, during or after an encounter with an assailant. The assailant counts on things going well for him during his attack. But if you scream, it is an immediate distraction. He must decide whether or not anyone will hear you and come to your aid. This divides his attention from the attack and introduces the element of fear into his own mind. Is it worth it to him to be caught or should he make a quick getaway and try again?

Of course, this defensive use of your voice only works in an area where some other people may be able to hear you. There is no point in screaming for help in a deserted forest.

There is an offensive use of the voice as well. Martial artists in many karate systems practice what is called a "kiai," or sudden, sharp shout. This is used to distract, startle and unnerve the opponent. It helps to confuse the senses so that your assailant cannot concentrate on what you are doing as well. The momentary shock of the sudden loud shout will actually freeze the person in place for an instant which helps you to deliver your counterattack successfully. It can also help you focus your energies on your own strike, so that it is done suddenly with full, explosive force. Your "kiai" helps you and hinders the assailant at the important moment that really counts. At that point, you are no longer a passive victim.

CHAPTER THREE

Tactics Against Locks, Holds and Chokes

Tactics Against Locks, Holds and Chokes

In many cases, if someone larger or stronger than you should surprise you by grabbing you in a lock or hold, your main problem might well be panic. What can you do? The mugger or assailant has a choke hold on you or he has applied a bear hug and is beginning to squeeze the breath from your body. What can you do?

The situation is probably not as serious as you think. Remain calm and recognize the fact that in many cases, the assailant is using both hands to choke or grab you. At least, he has not struck a vital organ or knocked you unconscious. You still have many weapons built into your body and the first step is to pick the weapon and the target. If the opponent is using both hands to grab you, he cannot use them to block your attack. He is also exposing a large area of his body, or perhaps, his face and head.

The following techniques will show some very simple ways to get out of trouble but you should also think about several principles that these various techniques employ. Then you will be free to improvise and flow with any emergency situation.

The first principle is not to waste strength wrestling with an opponent if he already has you at a disadvantage. Instead, look for a way to strike that will cause pain and shock first and then find a way to get out of his grip, choke or lock.

The second principle is to get your balance and maintain it. If you can maneuver the attacker off balance, his advantage will be neutralized effectively.

The third principle is to use your entire body weight in any movement or technique that you try. Don't just use your arm strength alone. Put your hips, legs and upper body behind each movement fully.

Finally, remember that the attacker is always vulnerable somewhere. Even if he is behind you, on top of you, and even if he is taller or bigger, he is still vulnerable to the right attack to the right target. Be calm and assess the situation and you will find a solution.

The following techniques are among the best ways to get out of locks and holds but they are not the only ways. Practice them with a partner, preferably with someone who is bigger and stronger than you, until you are confident that you can use them effectively. Make your moves smooth and sure so that you can do them without hesitation or thinking.

Two questions that might come to mind is why there has been such an emphasis on getting free from locks and holds and why so many kicking techniques are used.

The answer to the first question is that this is a book on self-defense intended for everyone; this means people who might be caught unaware by an attacker and find themselves in a difficult spot before they can act.

Being caught in a headlock or a choke can cause some panic, particularly if you have not practiced a couple of techniques that will work to free yourself from the attacker.

It is also important to strike effectively before the pressure from the lock or hold causes extreme pain or unconsciousness.

Many kicking techniques are shown for a number of reasons: 1) kicks are not usually expected. Most people think of fighting as something you do standing up facing your opponent using a boxing stance. 2) Your legs are longer and more powerful than your arms. If you can kick your opponent successfully, you will probably do more damage than you would using hand techniques. Women particularly can compensate for having less upper body strength than a man of the same general size by using strong, kicking moves. 3) Still another good reason is that it can be hard to defend against a good kick. Most people can instinctively duck a punch coming at their head but it is harder to get out of the way of a surprise kick.

It is important to practice the kicking movements and to be able to remain in balance when you execute them. If you kick out and lose your own balance, you have given up your advantage and put yourself in an even more dangerous predicament.

Here, the young lady is accosted on the street. Before she recognizes what the man's intentions are, he has grabbed her in a close embrace. He may be intent on rape or simply mauling her but she must react quickly.

Because both his arms are around her body, she has her hands free and he is exposed to her strike. She uses a strong palm heel thrust to the chin, driving his head back sharply. Note that she did not struggle to escape but chose an obvious target instead. This is a strong technique but it does not incapacitate the attacker. She must follow through with another move before she can escape.

The woman drives an elbow strike with her free left arm to the exposed throat of the attacker. Notice how well this move follows up on the thrust just before it. It is a natural and powerful movement that flows from the first technique. She has still not had to adjust her feet or body position but instead she has taken advantage of being held in closely by the assailant.

Before the assailant can recover, the woman gets away. She looks back to make sure he is not in pursuit. This attack to the throat can cause jamming of the windpipe and should only be used in case of real danger. Practice this technique without any contact and with extreme caution.

Here is another technique that can be used in the same situation. The man has accosted the young woman and grabs her around the waist. She grabs for the long hair at the back and sides of his head for a controlling grip before he realizes what is happening.

Pulling down and holding him in place, she prepares a knee to the groin. She drops her own weight back slightly for better balance, bringing the attacker slightly forward.

She makes sure the technique works by driving the knee high, and up, so that there is enough impact to completely disable the attacker. Done correctly, there would be no need for a follow-up technique in this case. If the knee does not work, the attacker's face is exposed at this point for another move. The technique is simple but that is one of its advantages.

Eric is standing when his attacker suddenly grabs him in a choke, threatening to strangle him. To demonstrate how simple a technique can be, Eric prepares to escape.

By simply turning his upper body completely in a sudden movement, Eric is free of the choke. Try it with a partner to convince yourself that it works. Eric is free but the assailant is still in contact and must be stopped.

Eric prepares a kick, sinking his weight onto the supporting leg and kicking to the extended, lead leg of his attacker.

Eric kicks out for the knee joint with a powerful thrust kick that buckles the lead leg. The attacker must fall while Eric concentrates on finishing the movement. Although the groin area was exposed as well, the higher kick always carries more danger to the kicker, since he will be vulnerable if he misses or is partially blocked in his attempt. Most people are not trained to anticipate a kick to the knee.

The attacker has grabbed Eric in a choke from the front. This attack leaves the assailant vulnerable in many ways. But it is the action of someone who has become suddenly enraged. His grip may be quite strong, whether he is big or not, if the adrenaline is flowing.

Eric drives a simple punch through the outstretched arms of the attacker to the chin. This might knock out the attacker but not necessarily. Eric did not have time to utilize much momentum so he will follow up.

Moving from the strike into his next counter, Eric breaks the grip on his throat by striking to the attacker's gripping arm with his right hand in a short, powerful motion.

Now he returns to strike back with an elbow to the face or throat with the same arm having used very economical movements to free himself and stop the attacker. Note the deep, powerful stance and balance Eric uses while executing the techniques.

Eric is standing on the street when the attacker makes his attempt to grab him. There are many techniques that could be used but this one illustrates the principle that the simplest, fastest and most powerful way to the target is best.

Eric simply launches a front snap kick to the groin.

The attacker, who is lunging forward, cannot recover in time to avoid the kick and is caught squarely. The kick is useful in that it protects Eric because the leg is longer than the arm reach of the attacker, and leg muscles are always more powerful than the arms.

The attacker grabs Eric's neck to get a lock on him or possibly knee him in the face. Eric finds himself held tightly by a bigger attacker.

Eric follows the movement of the attacker rather than struggling against it. He simply drops his head and upper body and comes out from under the grip. It is a simple technique but must be done quickly.

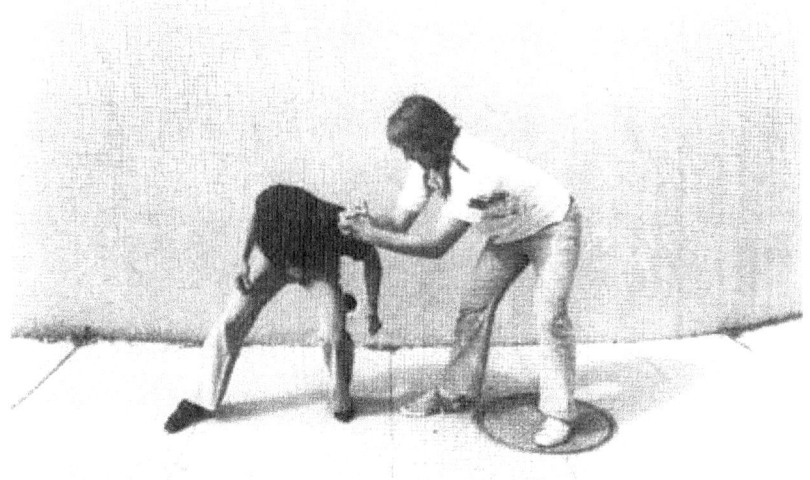

As Eric comes up in a circling motion he is already moving away from the attacker.

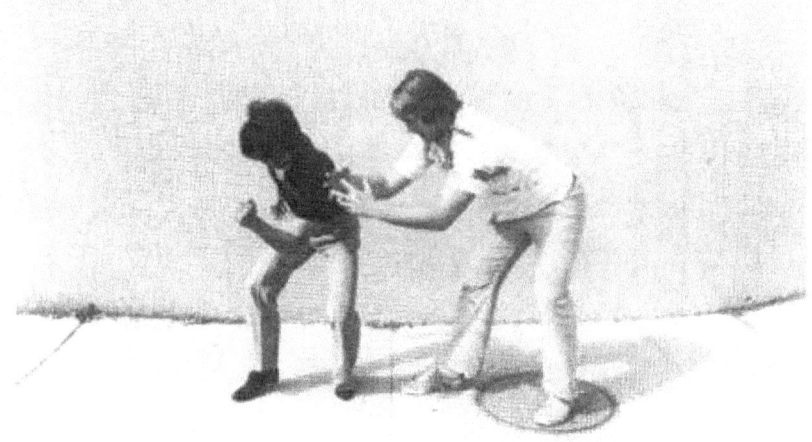

The attacker begins to follow up and reach for Eric, but Eric is moving quickly bringing his upper body and shoulder out of reach. More important, his weight has already shifted to his right foot, the one furthest away from the attacker.

Eric begins to launch a kick back at the attacker, who is still intent on reaching the upper body.

The kick is fully extended into the groin of the attacker. If the attacker had actually anticipated the kick and used his hands to block it, Eric could have straightened up and attacked the exposed face and head instead.

The same headlock is attempted here. Although it may not be common among trained fighters, a larger man will many times use his superior strength against a smaller man by attempting locks or punishing hold of this type.

Eric notes the distance between himself and the attacker as the hold is applied.

Eric senses the most direct opening available and launches a straight punch upward between the attacker's arms to his chin. (A woman may use a strike to the throat or solar plexes.)

Eric chooses a strike to the chin because it drives the head up and back, breaking the hold completely at the same time. If Eric wanted to follow up with a kick, the groin area is exposed to a knee or short snap kick.

Walking alone, Eric is attacked by a lone assailant from behind. There was no warning, so the attacker has been able to grab Eric and apply a choke with both hands.

Eric turns toward the assailant, shifting his entire body and maintaining a strong center of balance. Note how the position of the leg is identical to a formal "horse" stance. He prepares to counter at the same time that the turning motion has loosened the attacker's grip on his neck.

Eric swings his arm in a short arch upward and toward the attacker completely breaking his grip and pushing both arms to one side.

Eric traps the attacker's arms and immobilizes them with one arm, locking up the attacker, and cocking his free hand for a follow-up strike.

Eric strikes to the exposed neck of the attacker with his free hand.

The follow-through shows the power, driving the attacker backward. Note the perfect positioning of the legs and the rotation of the hips in conjunction with the strike. Eric has maximum leverage and complete control and balance.
Eric has taken control of the situation by maintaining good balance, and by combining his turning movement toward the attacker with a strike that breaks away the choke grip. He then ties up both attacker's arms with one arm leaving him one hand free to strike.

Here Eric has not tried to match upper body strength with an opponent who already has a secure lock on him. Instead, he goes toward the exposed facial area, exerting pressure where the opponent cannot resist. He must give way to pressure on the sensitive areas of the face, eyes and nose. The headlock has already been neutralized but not yet broken. By the time Eric has pulled the attacker backwards, a small amount of force has been enough to reverse the leverage and put Eric in control. He then launches the kick that will disable and overcome the attacker. Only after the attacker is completely at a disadvantage will Eric try to release the grip and at this point, the attacker would be trying to restore his own balance, if possible, and is unable to retain any of his grip at all.

The attacker begins with a headlock on Eric and applies pressure.

Eric reaches his free hand up to the head of the attacker from behind the shoulder.

He covers the face of the attacker with his hand, gripping the sensitive nose and eyes and pulling backwards sharply. At the same time, his left hand has been placed on the attacker's arm for balance and positioning.

Eric has reversed the situation, pulling the attacker back and completely off-balance while getting to a nearly erect position himself. The opponent has not loosened his grip around Eric's neck but it is no longer an effective attack. Eric launches a kick to the back of the knee.

Now Eric follows through with the kick while breaking the armlock on his neck with his left hand. The attacker is on his way to the ground.

Because this headlock position found Eric turned more toward his attacker and because the hip was not protecting the groin area, Eric struck to this vulnerable and open region. He follows with a complete attack to upper and lower parts of the body, arching the attacker's back and forcing him down and backward, breaking any last resistance by a kick to the back of the knee of the attacker. Now he can bring the opponent completely to the ground or strike into the exposed rib cage from his kneeling position.

Here again Eric is caught in a headlock. In this case the attacker's position leaves his groin area more exposed.

Eric uses the free left hand to punch into the groin area causing sudden and intense pain.

As the attacker reacts to the pain, Eric's rear hand comes up quickly in a natural arch.

Eric grips the attacker under the chin, keeping his balance centered and low. He pulls back sharply and starts to raise his upper body to an erect position.

As he reaches an erect, stable position, Eric brings the rear leg forward striking into the back of the attacker's knee with his own knee collapsing the leg. At the same time, Eric's left hand is pushing upwards on the locking arm around his neck.

The attacker's grip is broken, his head and neck are being forced backwards and the knee from behind has driven him from his feet to his knees. He is completely off-balance and vulnerable.

Eric uses the surprise of a kick to the knee to disable his attacker. While knee kicks are common to the martial arts, they are not used often in western fighting. This gives Eric the benefit of surprise. The inner side of the knee is extremely vulnerable to dislocation. Stepping on the foot adds still more pain and distraction in Eric's counterattack, allowing him the time he needs to move in and under the attacker, while loosening the lock. Once Eric has the attacker's arm leveraged over his own shoulder, the attacker cannot resist and he cannot use his free hand.

Eric is caught in a front headlock and unable to use his hands to much advantage.

Here he pulls slightly back from the attacker, placing his hand on the locking arm for contact.

Eric kicks unexpectedly to the exposed far knee, striking the vulnerable inside of the knee joint and damaging it.

Following this, Eric stomps downward to the same foot. He can "follow" the leg downward to the foot even if he cannot see it.

Now that the attacker is in extreme pain, Eric turns and moves under and out behind the attacker, grabbing the arm still wrapped around his neck.

Eric moves the foot from the attacker's foot and steps to the inside of his attacker, pivoting his upper body and bringing the gripping arm up and out, freeing himself. He now has a firm grip on the attacker's wrist and arm.

The attacker is now off-balance, stretched forward and held securely by one arm. He cannot bring the remaining arm, which is free, around into any kind of strike.

Eric brings the arm down over his knee, and the attacker is held helpless in an armlock.

Eric is grabbed from behind by the assailant in a choke hold. He will try to turn his head slightly and maintain a grip on the assailant's arm with his right hand to relieve any pressure on the Adam's apple. This will allow him time to take action. The Adam's apple should be fitted into the crook of the assailant's elbow so he cannot bring direct pressure that will cause unconsciousness.

Eric brings his free left hand up slightly to gain momentum in preparation to strike.

Eric strikes the groin with an elbow causing pain and shock that will either disable his assailant or permit him to free himself easily. Note how Eric has lowered his stance to be able to reach the groin easily and that he has used his entire upper body in launching the strike, adding to its power.

Eric breaks the grip of the choke arm while the assailant reacts to the initial groin strike. He is now free but still vulnerable to a counterattack by the assailant.

Eric prepares to finish the technique with a third move designed to stop the attacker completely.

Eric stomps on the attacker's foot, causing still more pain and allowing him time to move away easily.

Eric is again held in a choke hold from behind and demonstrates a slightly more advanced series of movements to disable the striker.

Eric grasps the choking arm of the attacker, turns his head into the crook of the arm to prevent loss of air and raises his foot in preparation to strike, all at the same time.

Eric stomps down on the foot, aiming, if possible, for the small toe, which is the most sensitive to pain. The shock of the pain allows Eric to break free of the choke arm and prepare a second attack to the upper body of the assailant.

Eric strikes with an elbow into the midsection or solar plexus, which will cause a temporary loss of oxygen and immobilize the attacker. In some cases, the attacker will collapse from this kind of strike. Once again, in demonstrating this technique Eric has used a pain attack to produce the shock and distraction that allows him to free himself from a locking hold and to follow up with a second strike to disable or stop his opponent.

Eric is held from behind in a bear hug. This type of locking hold is usually favored by large, powerful men who have confidence in their upper body strength. To try to match strength with someone like this is not generally the best strategy since they already have an initial advantage.

Eric uses his flexibility and the element of surprise to rotate his upper body and strike to the attacker's face with his elbow. The attacker is driven back and off-balance by the pain.

Before the attacker can recover, Eric rotates again to the opposite side gaining momentum for his follow-up strike.

Eric drives his other elbow into the midsection or solar plexus of the attacker from the left which forces the opponent to release his grip on him. Eric is free to continue in a natural and spontaneous way.

Eric moves his left foot in closer to the opponent's right foot so that he is now facing his attacker and maintaining good balance.

Eric drives a knee into the groin area finishing the series of three strikes that have attacked face, upper body and groin in a rapid series of simple, natural but effective movements.

Here Eric is held in a bear hug from behind. He shows an alternative approach to getting free which might be used if the attacker is holding the victim in a very rigid and restrictive grip making rotating the upper body difficult.

Eric senses that he cannot get his body and arm rotating into a strike to the face. He grabs the attacker's arm for some contact and leverage preparing to use a weapon that is not anticipated. Meanwhile, he brings his left hand around and under the attacker's grip to the handlock held by the attacker.

Eric suddenly strikes upward with his head contacting the attacker's face or chin and causing sudden pain and shock.

While the attacker is recovering, Eric turns his attention to the attacker's grip, grasping one or more fingers on the locking hand and prying them open, breaking the grip. He could not attempt this if he had not first attacked some other area of the body.

Eric has grasped the attacker's hand and forced it back and down in a painful manner. The attacker must follow the hand or have it broken at the wrist. Note how Eric has lowered his stance instinctively providing better balance and upsetting the attacker's balance at the same time.

Eric is now almost "sitting" in a deep stance and leveraging the opponent's arm over his outstretched upper leg. Now both the wrist and the elbow are under stress and the opponent is completely off balance and on his way backwards to the ground.

The opponent is helpless, his arm is held in a lock and his own right leg folded under him as he lies almost completely on his back.

Eric is held in a full Nelson lock which brings pressure to bear on the vertebrae of the neck. If enough pressure is used, the neck can be snapped forward and broken.

Eric quickly rotates his upper body just slightly to the left relieving the immediate, direct pressure of the lock. This move also opens up enough space to launch a strike. He raises his leg to kick out at his attacker.

Eric kicks to the inside of the knee joint, a particularly vulnerable area. This kick would usually break or dislocate the knee joint and cause severe pain.

Eric raises both hands to grip the attacker's lock, as the attacker feels his legs buckle from the strike.

Eric grasps one hand by the fingers and brings it down in an arch in front of him. The hand is forced back by the pressure on all the finger joints and the wrist.

Eric grips the other hand and brings it down also. He now has a controlling pain hold on both hands and is holding the attacker immobile. Eric's legs both act as a fulcrum for his controlling leverage.

Eric prepares to finish the attacker by a sudden elbow strike to the face.

Eric drives the elbow into the attacker, which will force him back and down allowing Eric to move away easily.

Eric has just left the building behind him and is headed toward his car when an attacker approaches on the street and grabs him by one arm.

Eric turns slightly toward the attacker, which loosens the tension between the attacker's arm and Eric's, and gives Eric a little room to move. He notes the position of the attacker's grip on his wrist.

Eric turns his hand palm down and pulls sharply and quickly free, working against the point where the thumb and forefinger meet in the grip. Although this is a simple technique, it works. The movement must be sudden and catch the opponent by surprise.

Before the attacker can recover, Eric kicks back sharply to the knee. This should prevent the attacker from pursuing the victim.

Eric demonstrates another variation on a one-handed grab escape. He pulls free by exerting force against the thumb-forefinger grip quickly and suddenly.

Before the attacker can decide what to do, Eric prepares a counter-attack.

Eric drives a kick into the groin, disabling the attacker.

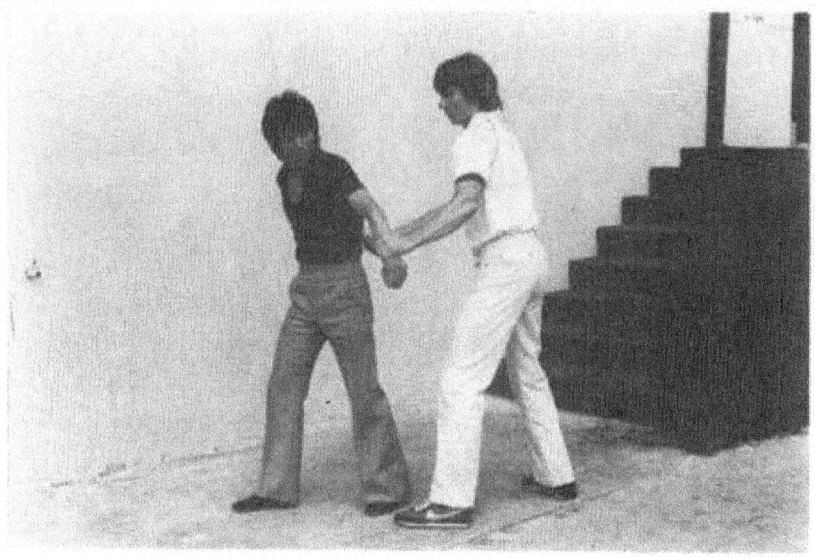

In this attack, Eric is grabbed from behind by both wrists. Although he could easily use a kick to start his counter-attack, he will show another way to get out of this kind of hold.

Here Eric turns toward his attacker moving his entire body including his foot position and rotating his upper body quickly and strongly.

This movement forces the attacker's arms against each other, freeing Eric's inside (right) hand. Speed and smooth rotation of the entire body are necessary to break through the hand grip of the attacker. Hesitation will allow the attacker to adjust to the force of the counter.

Rear view of hand release.

Now with one hand free, Eric strikes upward to the attacker's head before he can defend himself.

The strike is a palm heel thrust under the chin or to the lower part of the face which drives the attacker back and away.

Here is an alternate way of handling the same kind of hold on both wrists.

Eric steps back with the left leg getting a strong position inside the opponent's stance and allowing him to face the attacker. At the same time, he rotates the upper body jamming the attacker's arms together and loosening his grip and eliminating any leverage the attacker might have had.

Seen from the opposite side, the turning movement executed correctly and automatically frees the right hand from the attacker's grip and positions it for the technique that will follow.

This time, instead of striking up to the face, Eric brings the right hand into contact with the attacker's elbow, and shoves it up and around in an arch.

Eric maintains his leverage on the elbow, pushing it over and down, forcing the attacker to rotate and bend with the movement. The attacker's grasp on Eric's left hand has allowed Eric to maintain contact and hold on to that hand instead, allowing him to smash his head to the ground.

Eric holds the attacker so that he is in no danger of counterattack from the opponent. The flow of movement is simple and natural but practice is necessary to insure that the transfer of grips is made easily and the movement is circular following the natural contours of the attacker's body.

Summary

It stands to reason that if you are stronger and bigger than someone, they probably will not attack you and try to grab or choke you into unconsciousness. But anger or strong emotion may prompt someone to try just that. And even if an attacker happens to be bigger or stronger than you are and they have already gotten a choke, lock or hold on you, they are still vulnerable to a counterattack.

Try to remain calm and find the vulnerable target for your technique. It may be a simple kick to the groin or it may be a series of movements that will turn the tables on your attacker. Try to strike for pain and shock value. Try to maintain your balance instead of striking from an off-balanced position. Try to unbalance your attacker. Follow up your attack so that you can get away completely and safely.

Practice the techniques until they become a habit and you do not have to remember them or think about them. Practice with a taller or stronger partner if possible. Don't use half-hearted techniques; put your entire body into each movement and make your moves smooth and sure.

CHAPTER FOUR

Situational Self-Defense

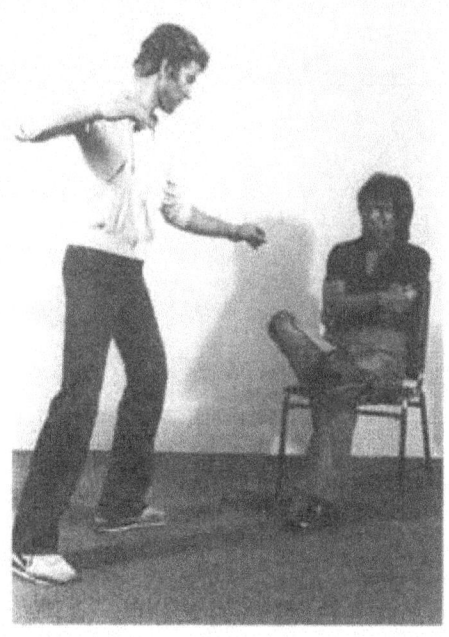

Eric is seated in a chair as the attacker approaches and prepares to punch him. This could take place in a restaurant, in a bus station, on a park bench or anywhere else. Although the victim might feel vulnerable because he is sitting and his attacker is on his feet, the response is simple.

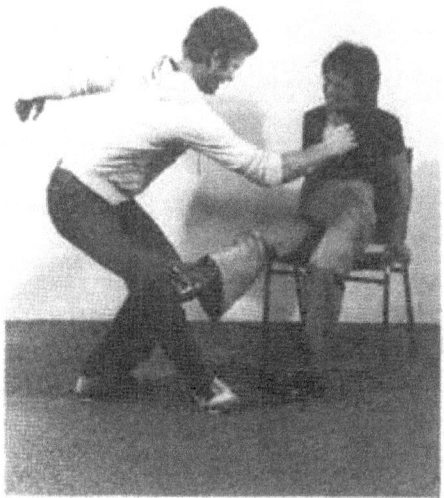

Eric thrust a kick to the knee of the advanced leg of the attacker. The pain will stop the attacker. The kick might well damage the knee since the attacker's full weight is on it. The chair is used as a brace and it is a solid support for this kind of a counter.

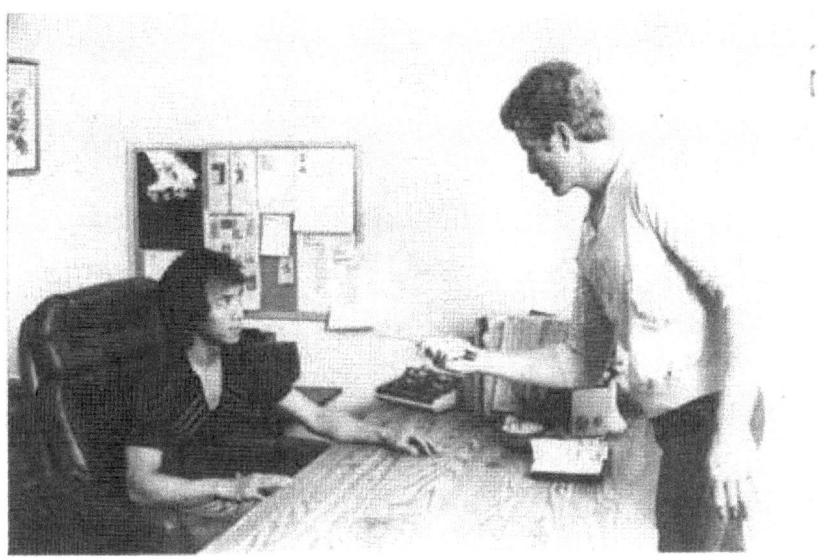

Eric is seated behind a desk when an assailant threatens him with a knife.

As the assailant thrusts the knife toward Eric, he parries it to the outside with one hand, leaving one hand free to follow up. Note that he has moved his assailant out and away from his own body, so that the assailant's remaining hand is not in line with his body and is useless at this moment.

Eric brings his other hand into play, grabbing the assailant's knife hand at the wrist firmly so that he has complete control and the weapon cannot be brought back in a return motion to injure him.

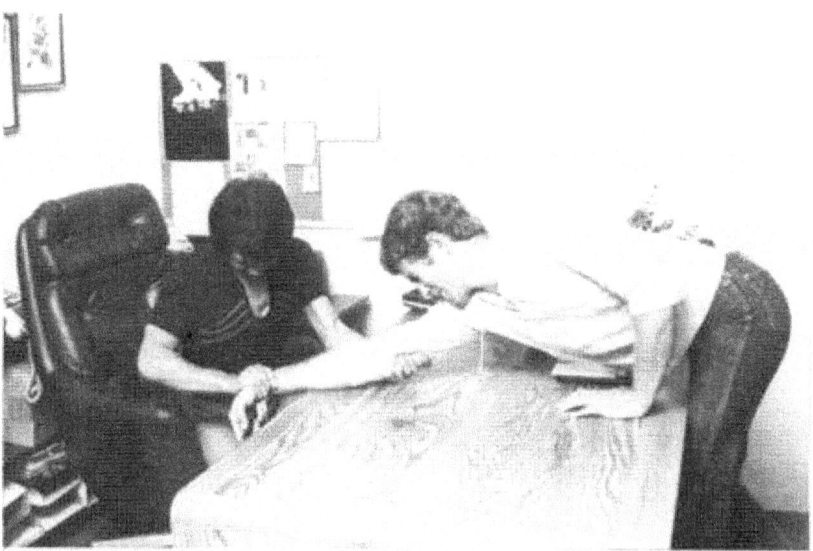

Eric brings the attacker's arm down suddenly and sharply on the desk top, forcing the knife from his hand and damaging his arm. The opponent is off balance because he is stretched out across the top of the desk surface.

Eric rises and moves directly with an elbow strike to the exposed face of the attacker. Note that this is the shortest, most direct route to a counter attack with the arm closest to the opponent and the target. Also note that Eric drives the elbow with full weight from the legs as well as from his torso for maximum power. Eric's left hand still maintains a grip on the attacker's wrist.

In a natural return motion, almost as though he were calmly sitting back down in the chair, Eric grabs the attacker's hair with the right hand, moves back and pulls the attacker's head forward and down.

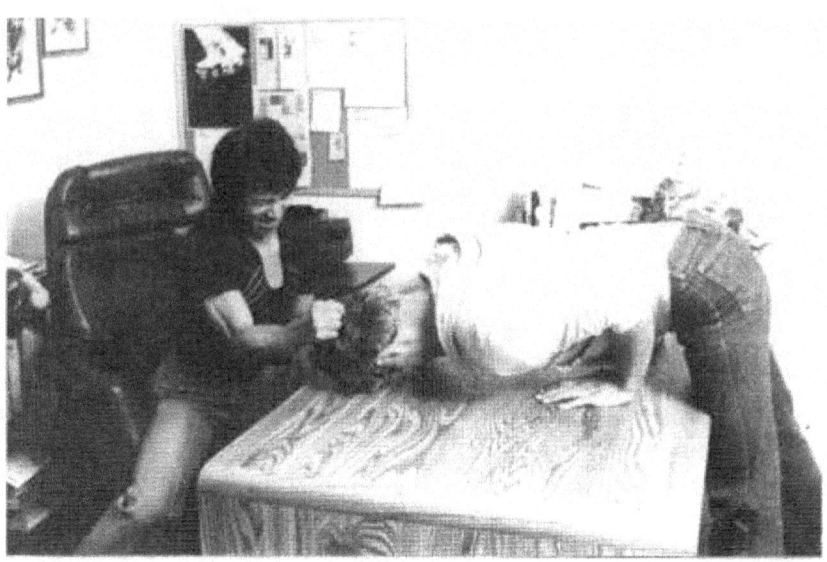

He strikes the attacker's face into the desk top, disabling him completely. Eric has used the surface of the desk as a weapon in his own defense twice in three moves, and allowed the width of the desk to keep the attacker off balance and overextended during his attack.

Eric is sitting on the ground in a park when the attacker approaches and threatens him. Eric is already braced on one arm as he notes the speed and direction of the oncoming punch.

Eric does not try to get up or he will be bowled over and perhaps hit as well. He doesn't try to roll away because he is in position to strike right now.

The kick to the inside of the knee will topple the attacker. The lead leg of the attacker presents the target and Eric's leg is longer than his attacker's arm which gives him the advantage of reach.

The young lady is sitting on a park bench, or it might be a bus stop just as easily, when the man sits down and begins to harass her, putting his arm around her shoulders.

She draws back her right arm and strikes with an elbow into the ribcage quickly, which doubles the attacker over.

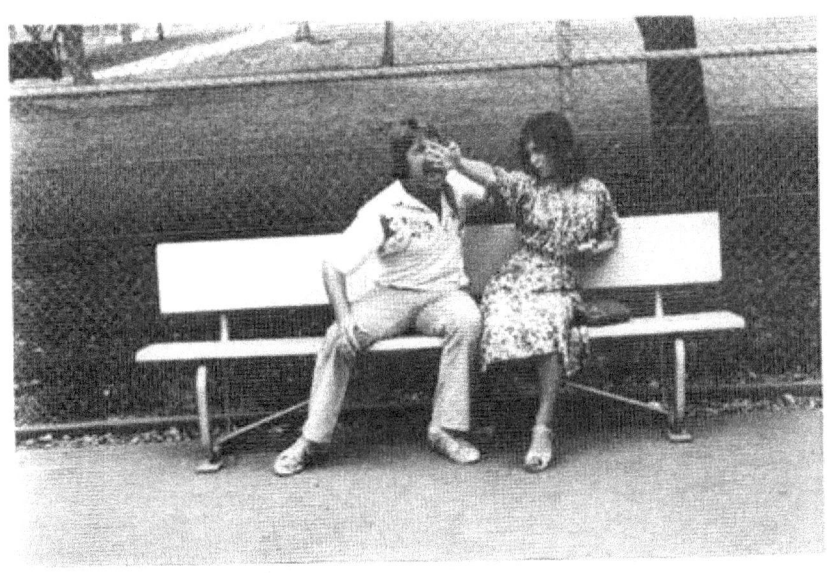

Using the inside hand again, she strikes to the eyes, temporarily blinding the attacker and stunning him as well.

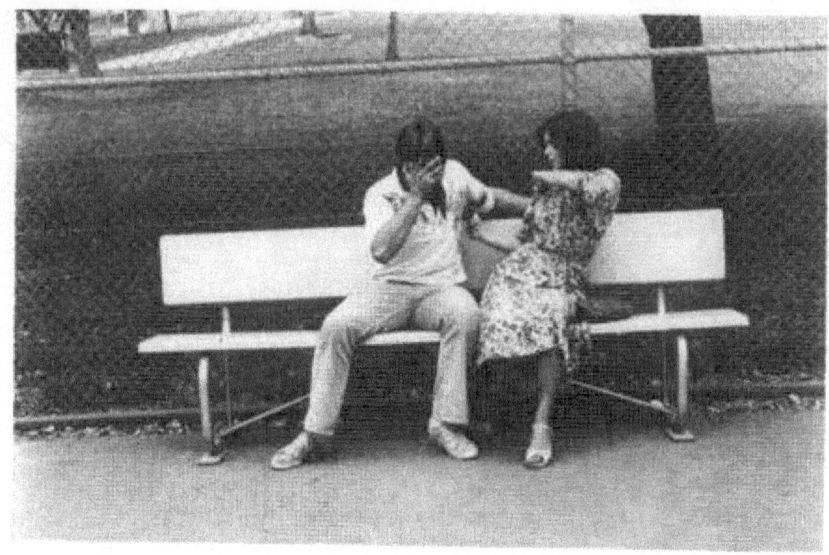

The woman rotates her upper body to face the attacker before he can recover, bringing her left arm up and into action. The movement loosens his arm from her shoulder.

She uses her right arm and hand to bring his arm up and over her head to the front also grabbing his arm with her left hand and getting a secure grip.

She stands, extending his arm with her left hand grip and bringing the right hand down smashing the elbow.

Now she brings her arm down in a short, sharp arch while placing her right hand on the elbow to exert pressure on the joint and maintain leverage. He is forced forward by the pain.

He is driven forward and down from the bench and she is free to escape.

Eric is on a corner with a newspaper when he is approached by the assailant. Perhaps an argument or an occasion where the individual has been drinking prompts the attack. The situation has only two unusual factors; Eric has a newspaper and there is a wall next to him.

The attacker moves in and Eric begins to use the newspaper as an improvised weapon.

Eric brings the newspaper up in a sweeping strike to the face and eyes of the attacker. Rolled up, the newspaper is stiff enough to cause pain and shock.

Eric follows through and the attacker is stunned momentarily and his head is pushed to the right by the impact.

Eric keeps his eyes on the attacker and begins to ready his other hand for a follow-up move. Note how his body weight has pivoted with the strike and how he remains on balance, facing his attacker.

Eric grabs the attacker's hair with the left hand since that is the nearest controlling move that he can do. His hand is cocked to strike again but the newspaper will not do any damage to the back of the attacker.

Eric drives the attacker into the wall with a push. This will injure the attacker and Eric is now completely in control. The element of surprise was the main factor in making this technique effective. The use of the two elements that were available is typical of someone who has the confidence to take advantage of his environment.

The young lady is making a telephone call in a public phone booth when the attacker approaches. She sees he will not back off and she feels trapped, but she is not. She could slam the door on him but that leaves him outside and angry while she is still inside.

Using the phone, she strikes to the face or head with the receiver in a suprise move.

She makes sure to follow up with still another sudden attack by using a sharp elbow strike to the midsection.

Before the man can recover, she has slipped by him and is on her way to safety at full speed. A phone receiver or any other object made of hard plastic can become a weapon if needed. It is usually better to strike with some kind of hard, improvised weapon than with just a bare hand.

Summary

The techniques shown in this chapter can be applied in many ways and in a variety of situations. They are not just rigid moves to be memorized. They should be understood so that you can use them at will.

A technique demonstrated earlier in the book showing a rape attack is not just a defense against rape. The woman on the ground held down by the attacker might just have well have been a man held down by another on a barroom floor. The same principles that make the techniques work in one situation will apply in another.

A technique shown on a chair can be used on a bench, but the reason why the technique works should be studied. Work with a partner and try to simulate real situations. Go to a park, a bench, a phone booth, or an alley. Let your partner work out an attack and surprise you. Test your awareness, your presence of mind and your execution.

While the techniques vary and will work in many places, there are certain factors that make each technique work that cannot be changed. You can't do a technique off balance, with the wrong hand moving first, and so on. Experiment with them and they will become real to you. In this way, you can come to appreciate them and you will gain confidence in your ability to make these practical techniques work for you.

CHAPTER FIVE

Special Problems: Under Attack,
Weapons, More Than One Attacker

Special Problems

Instead of learning a wide range of specific defenses for specific attacks, leave it open. Use whatever technique comes to you naturally in a given situation. This will prevent you from memorizing rigid patterns. The problem with pre-set patterns is that conflicts in real life never seem to fit the pattern. You are then at a loss as to how to act.

Try to become flexible and learn to fit the action you take to the circumstances as they arise. The advantage of learning to react in this flexible way is that you don't have to stop to think and you can act immediately.

There is some argument among people in the martial arts about the value of traditional training versus the modern approach. I feel there is value in both. This book is a reference work and if you are a martial artist you can gain something by using it. If you have no experience, it can help you begin to get some training and knowledge. There are many kinds of martial arts schools; some concentrate on forms, some on self-defense and some on health and philosophy. My view is "to each his own." What you think you need is what you should pursue.

This book offers only a moderate number of techniques but they are among the most effective in real encounters. If we demonstrated two hundred techniques, it would take you too long to master them. Practice, learn and master a few. One technique mastered is better than one hundred techniques barely known.

Beyond this, one technique can be applied to many situations and you must learn how to adapt it in this way. Experiment and use your awareness and you'll be surprised at what you will discover.

The following techniques are shown in particular situations. The intended victim is already under attack from a punch or kick or he is facing a knife, club, or other lethal weapon, or he is facing more than one attacker. These techniques should help you see how to flow with the situation effectively.

Eric is approached by the assailant and recognizes that he is under attack.

The attacker does the unexpected and prepares a front snap kick instead of using his hands.

By moving quickly in a diagonal line, Eric avoids the kick and comes in close to his attacker. Both men are moving forward fairly rapidly.

As the attacker is carried forward by his momentum, Eric prepares to counter. Because both men are roughly side to side, Eric does not have a ready opening for a hand technique that is simple to execute. He begins a kick that will take advantage of the unusual position he is in.

Eric kicks down to the back of the knee of the attacker bending the leg and forcing the opponent to fall as seen in the photo. This is a good example of taking advantage of the situation instead of having some kind of planned technique in mind. Real life conflict brings up unorthodox situations that call for the ability to be flexible and adaptable.

An attack with a knife has forced Eric to react quickly and instinctively. He avoids the knife thrust by stepping to one side and moving his body out of the direct line of attack.

He grabs the knife hand with his right hand which will prevent the attacker from cutting back toward him immediately. Now the attacker is neutralized but Eric must quickly start his counterattack.

Eric grabs the knife hand with his left hand while stepping across in front of the attacker at the same time. The upward movement of the arms is coordinated with the one step forward with the left foot.

Eric now brings the attacker's arm down in a forward arch while settling into a strong stance. This levers the attacker's arm over Eric's shoulder. The attacker is completely off-balance and forced to drop the knife. Smooth execution and speed are imporant so that the movement becomes one, complete and coordinated technique that can be done instinctively and quickly. Hesitation allows the attacker to feel for an advantage and react against the counterattack.

In this case, Eric is threatened with a knife again. But there is an important difference in this situation that prompts him to use another technique for self-defense. In this case, the knife is held much higher and closer to the face of the victim. Eric could not step in and make the same moves with both hands as he did in the previous situation . . . a new technique is necessary.

Eric brings both hands up and across his body, the left hand deflecting the knife out and away from him for immediate protection. The right hand snaps forward in a very fast back slap into the eyes of the attacker. This is not a heavy strike or punch. It is designed to sting and distract the opponent by pain.

Eric again seizes the weapon hand in both of his hands with a firm grip and starts to maneuver the knife hand in an arch.

Eric is on balance and controlling the knife, the blade's cutting edge is now away from him and moving up.

Eric takes a step forward while continuing the arch upwards with both hands, taking the assailant completely off balance by stretching him up and turning the arm out.

Eric brings the knife arm around and down while stepping back with his left foot. This move needs practice but is fairly simple to do. Eric is now beside the attacker and slightly to the rear as the knife continues down in its path.

Eric drops into a low stance as he concludes the entire movement which drives the knife into the assailant who has had no real chance to anticipate the technique or interrupt it once it was under way. Eric has used movement and body weight to reverse the situation as well as the element of surprise. Smooth execution and proper body positioning is required to make this technique effective.

The assailant approaches to attack the victim with a stick, club or any other weapon using an overhead strike. Obviously the attack is already underway as Eric assesses the direction and speed of the assailant.

Eric steps slightly to one side while moving his upper body and head out of the direct line of attack. This gives him time to maneuver and take advantage of the attacker's momentum. Eric opens one hand for a parry to the weapon arm.

Eric sweeps across to block and redirect the attacker's weapon hand controlling its direction and preventing any kind of return strike that the attacker might try.

Eric continues his own blocking movement downward, forcing the attacker forward and slightly off balance. This move takes advantage of the momentum that the attacker had initiated by his own strike. This move does not block with force against force. In this way, it does not matter if the attacker might be bigger or physically stronger than the victim. Eric prepares to counter-attack.

By rotating his upper body as he blocked downward, Eric is automatically in position to strike back and up to the exposed face and head of the attacker. A strong palm heel thrust to the face or chin will drive the attacker back in pain.

The assailant launches an attack against the victim again using an overhead strike with a stick or club. Note that Eric does not telegraph what he will do. He is poised as though he might retreat.

Instead, Eric steps in closer and brings his left arm up in a block on the forearm of the assailant. This block uses the arm nearest to the attacking arm and leaves the remaining hand free to deal with the assailant's free hand. The attack has been completely neutralized already. Note that Eric stepped in closer to the threat rather than backing away, although the instinctive thing to do is step away. This is actually safer than trying to flee from the attacker.

Eric allows his blocking hand to remain loose and in contact with the assailant's arm, and he begins to launch a kick to the vulnerable inside of the knee. This is more effective than punching with his free hand because the attacker cannot block the kick and he does not have time to get his weight off the lead left leg.

The leg buckles out unbalancing the attacker and causing serious pain. This prevents the attacker from using his free hand or recovering his balance.

Eric prepares to launch a strike to the open, upper body or face of the attacker and steps in close to maintain his center of balance. He begins to launch the strike. The opponent is too close for a full swing. A normal punch would be blocked by the free left hand, so Eric drives an elbow strike to the throat which has a shorter arch and reaches the target sooner. Meanwhile, Eric's left arm has looped around the attacker's right arm and holds it locked. The weapon is useless.

In a follow-up movement, Eric brings the right hand back from the elbow strike and catches the attacker's hair and grips it firmly. He then yanks the attacker's hair and grips it firmly. He then yanks the attacker to the ground for a complete takedown. This insures that he is in control even if the elbow blow did not do serious damage. Note how the moves follow one another quickly and naturally, not allowing the attacker a chance to regroup or counter.

The attacker again approaches with an overhead strike. Eric demonstrates an alternate technique for more experienced people. He is prepared to move but shows no sign of how he will counter.

Eric uses a double handed block against the descending club which is strong enough to fully block this strike. Eric then grips the attacker's wrist with his left hand.

Eric twists the attacker's hand out and around in a short circle bringing his left hand and arm around and down lowering his whole body for added power.

Eric continues moving his left hand, which controls the attacker's weapon hand in an arch. He rotates his upper body to the inside to maintain power and momentum. The attacker is now being forced by the leverage and the pressure on his wrist and elbow. He must follow the line of the movement. His upper body is already being moved off balance and out of his own control. The pressure exerted by Eric prevents the attacker from using the free hand.

Eric uses his free hand to pry the club loose. His left hand has a pain hold on the opponent who cannot maintain a strong grip on the weapon.

With the weapon in his own hand, Eric thrusts straight into the target, the attacker's solar plexus. This strike can stun and cause temporary paralysis.

Eric moves from the first thrust without drawing back the club. He simply sweeps it straight upward across the face of the attacker in a vertical line.

Before the attacker can recover, if he will recover at all, Eric sweeps downward in a smooth arch and rakes the club across the attacker's shins, producing more pain and further disabling the attacker.

The attacker strikes at the victim with a bottle as his weapon. If he picks up a bottle at all, it is likely that the angered attacker will strike in this way instinctively.

Eric moves quickly to one side avoiding the downward sweep of the bottle and raising his arms to protect his upper body in preparation for the attacker's next move.

The attacker's momentum has carried his strike all the way down to his knee level and now he will try to recover and attack again.

The attacker sweeps a backhand strike toward Eric who is now on the attacker's right side. Eric has raised his arm in preparation to block this strike.

Eric steps forward and blocks the backhand swing at the same time, using both arms in a vertical double block. But the right hand at the attacker's wrist will grab for a hold to control the bottle.

Eric pulls the attacker's arm slightly from the wrist and cocks the left arm ready to strike into the opponent.

Without taking time to move his feet or change position, Eric drives a back hand strike up the arm and into the throat of the attacker.

As he follows through, Eric steps forward with his left foot so that he is slightly in front of the attacker. Now maintaining a strong grip on the bottle hand, he drives the attacker back and down by sinking his body as he maintains pressure on the throat and arm. Eric's front leg becomes the fulcrum point over which the attacker is leveraged. Eric is half-kneeling but the opponent is doubled over backwards, one leg folded under him and without the ability to move or get up. The key to the takedown and control of the attacker is the step forward with the left foot which shifts the positions of the two men relative to one another.

The attacker launches a punch to the victim's face from a straight frontal position. This is typical of many fighting situations.

The simplest way is the best way. Eric steps in. He shifts his upper body just slightly to one side, slipping in the punch, and strikes straight up to the face with a counter punch. Eric's left hand can cover or deflect the first punch if the timing is not quite so effective. Speed, surprise and timing make this simple technique work.

This is a common situation in the case of an argument between two people. The attacker draws back the right hand to punch for the face of the victim. An angered person will usually go for this kind of attack. The problem for the attacker is that in cocking his arm to throw the punch, he telegraphs his plan to the victim.

Eric shifts his weight to the far foot and draws up for a side kick into the lower body area. Again, this is a simple counter that takes advantage of the distance and the exposed lower body. There is no real need to block the punch or move away.

The fully extended kick catches the attacker in the abdomen and illustrates the obvious truth that the leg is longer than the arm. Good balance and practice is required to master controlled kicking. With a little practice, the simple kicks to knees and groin are invaluable weapons. High kicks are dangerous for anyone but the very experienced martial artists.

Danger of Weapons and Multiple Attackers

When you are under attack by more than one person, try to maneuver yourself so that the attackers are grouped together in a line. Therefore, you do not face more than one of them at any one time. If possible, try to throw or push one attacker into another or use one to block the progress or attack of another. Try to get your back to a wall so that you cannot be approached from the back and the front at the same time. Even if you cannot do the things described, the situation is not necessarily hopeless. Here are some examples of successful defense against more than one attacker.

Eric has already been grabbed by both wrists by the attacker in front of him while, at the same time, another attacker is beginning to choke him from behind.

Eric steps forward slightly and drives one elbow up into the face of the first attacker. This stuns the attacker for the moment and, at the same time, forces one of his arms into the other sharply breaking his grip on Eric's right wrist.

Eric cocks the right arm, just freed from the first attacker's grasp for a return strike. Eric's movement to the right, with his entire upper body, has weakened the grasp of the man behind attempting to choke him. This man's leverage is no longer as effective as it was.

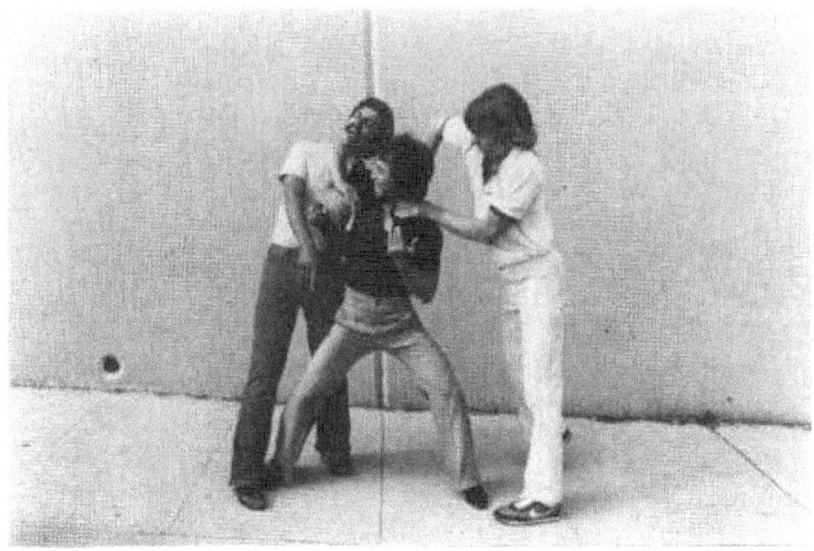

Eric drives the right arm back into the first attacker's face or throat breaking his hold completely and causing severe pain. Eric's movement back and forth continues to weaken the choke hold of the second attacker.

Eric spins to the left now to deal with the second attacker. The choke hold position of this attacker's arms prevents an effective elbow strike to the face or chest. Eric swings his arms up slightly.

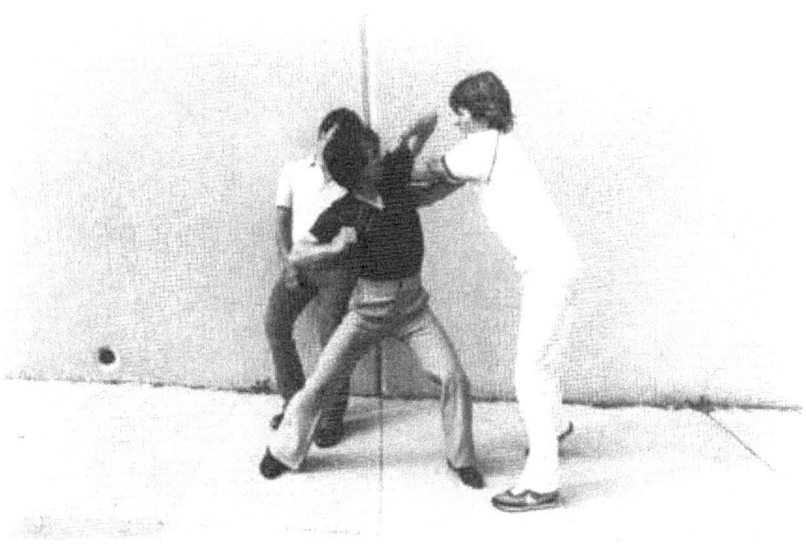

Eric's arm swings over the choke hold breaking free of the grip of the second man who is also distracted by the arm and fist moving past his face.

Eric allows his moving left arm to wrap around both arms of the second man trapping them. He still has one hand completely free.

Eric uses a natural motion to follow through on his own momentum and drive a punch straight to the face of the second man.

Eric completes the strike with a full body follow through to produce enough power to drive the attacker back. He is free to escape before anyone can recover.

Here Eric is grabbed from the front and the back by two assailants, who try to get a hold on his arms.

Eric starts to counterattack immediately since both men are in so close. He draws up his leg for a downward thrust but not to the toes as in the earlier technique.

Eric again attacks the vulnerable knee joint of the right side attacker. If he can break or dislocate the knee, the pain will stop the man and prevent him from moving or pursuing Eric at all.

Without stopping, Eric returns the same leg in a knee strike to the groin of the other attacker. The economy of action in this technique prevents the second man from getting to him in time. Note that once again Eric has not stepped down from one attack and then launched a second strike . . . he has moved immediately from one to another in a return motion while his weight remains on the same leg.

Eric is held from behind in a choke while a second assailant approaches from the front and tries to punch him in the midsection.

Eric grabs the choking arm with both hands and draws up his leg for a kick. The second attacker launches a punch.

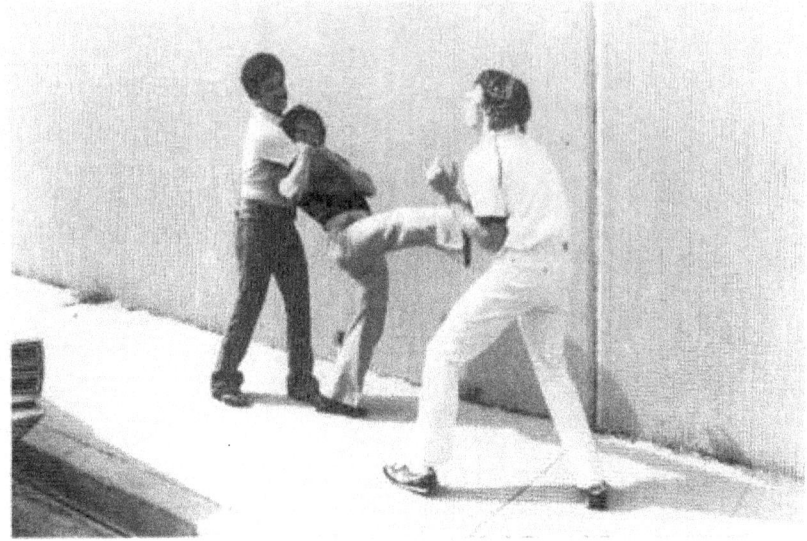

Eric drives a front kick to the groin or stomach of the attacker before the punch can reach the target. He has used the longer reach of his leg to good advantage.

As the first attacker doubles up in pain, Eric begins to work on getting free. He pulls downward on the choking arm and launches a stomp to the foot of the man holding him. This strike does not require that Eric change his position or balance or use his strength against the attacker holding him.

As the pain registers on the attacker, Eric uses the same leg to step slightly outside the attacker and begins to lower his stance and pull his opponent over his outstretched leg in a simple hip throw.

The attacker is put off-balance and thrown over the tripping leg to the ground.

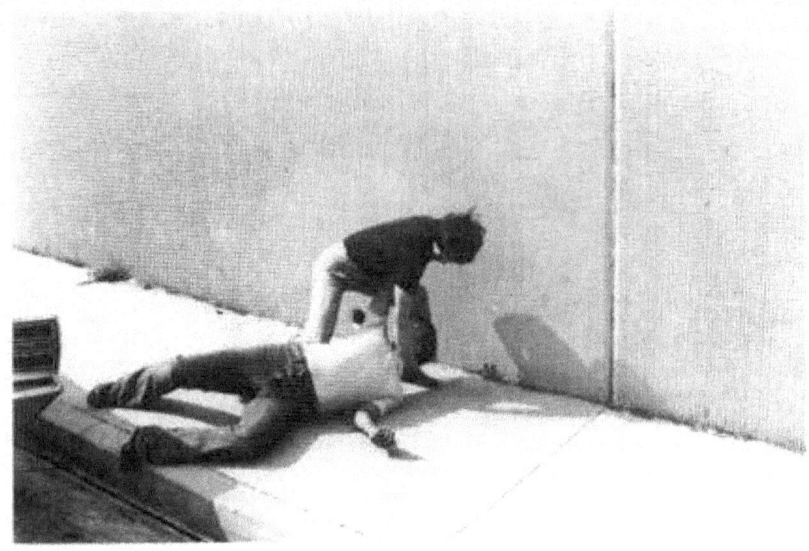

The attacker hits the pavement.

Eric is caught by two attackers, one on each side of him. They are grabbing both arms by the wrist to prevent his punching either one of them.

Eric uses both attackers for balance and starts a kick back to the right side attacker.

Rather than try a high kick, Eric goes for the inside of the knee joint buckling the attacker's leg under him.

Because time is so important before either attacker can react, Eric swings a sweep kick into the remaining attacker.

The full impact of the kick drives the second man back into the wall.

Eric is trapped between two attackers who approach him.

Eric sidesteps and avoids the rush of the first attacker who is caught slightly off guard.

By rotating quickly but without changing his foot position, Eric drives his hands to the head of the attacker and bangs him into the wall.

Without changing his hand position, Eric now grabs the man's hair and pulls him down slightly while simultaneously driving his knee to the groin or midsection. The second attacker is nearly upon him.

Without lowering his leg from its raised position, Eric prepares to kick the second attacker.

Eric kicks to the stomach or groin of the second man, still maintaining his control on the first attacker who is stunned and helpless. Again the movement is made from strike to strike without pause or hesitation.

Eric is still in control as the second man doubles under the impact.

Summary

To be effective your techniques must be delivered with power. Making your body work is like the torque created by an engine. It starts at your feet, moves through the legs, then the hips, to shoulders, arms and hands. They must all move together in one explosive instant.

You cannot arm punch someone and expect it to be effective. Your whole body must be behind your strike. In this way, even a physically weaker or smaller person can have real power. Bruce Lee was a great example of this because of his size. The bigger person has his body weight on his side but he may never learn how to really produce power effectively. Speed becomes power upon impact. That is why power is a combination of your entire body moving in one, explosive moment.

To handle a special problem calls for more confidence than usual and there is less room for an error in technique. Practicing correct body position, speed and follow-through are even more important in this kind of situation. But the attacker with the weapon may be fearful once his advantage is neutralized. The attack by more than one person can sometimes be stopped by picking out the obvious leader and striking at him suddenly and strongly. Just as in the case of locks and holds, there is always a way to gain control of the situation.

CHAPTER SIX

BODY TONING TECHNIQUES

Body Toning Techniques

Practice is an important element in achieving success and there are some vital points to remember about practicing correctly. Correct mental practice includes visualizing a situation. This mental preparation increases your concentration and creativity. You must understand the techniques both mentally and physically. Review and reflect on what you have learned constantly.

At the same time, mental practice without physical training means you won't have either timing or conditioning. Time and effort is a requirement in practicing these techniques even though many of them are simple. First learn the movement physically and then try to understand how it works. Psychologically, this becomes a part of your learning experience. After a certain point, you can become creative and versatile with the techniques, Then experimenting becomes the continued process of learning.

Often, it helps to find a partner so that you encourage each other to practice regularly. After some time is spent in training, you will find it easier to enjoy the learning experience involved in the techniques.

This book has some of the best and simplest techniques for beginners, as well as advanced combinations for trained martial artists, but you must practice until you can do them without hesitation. This kind of practice can help you gain confidence and overcome fear.

EXERCISES FOR WARMING UP

Although it is natural to be eager to practice the techniques for self-defense, it is important to begin training sessions with a warmup. The exercises shown here will enable you to warmup and to develop your entire body in a progressive way. The exercises not only warm you up but they help you to do the techniques more effectively. In addition, they greatly reduce the chance of injury during practice.

How long is a good warmup? Professional ballet dancers warm up for two hours before going on stage to perform. You should develop your own sense of the right amount of warmup time. A rule of thumb might be a minimum of fifteen minutes for an hour of practice. More warmup is better if you devote more time to training.

A good warmup is more than just stretching . . . it means warming up your body. Jumping is warming up, running is warming up and stretching is warming up.

Make sure that your practice space is clear and that there are no objects that might trip or injure you. The room you use should be at normal temperature. Sweatsuits are a good idea and in colder weather the leg warmers used by dancers are helpful. Never begin punching or kicking techniques when you are cold or stiff.

Three Basic Warmup Exercises

JUMPING JACKS

Jumping jacks are a simple way to increase cardiovascular functioning and they are familiar to most of us.

Stand erect with your feet together and your arms at your sides. Jump up and extend your feet to the sides to about shoulder width and bring your arms up from your sides to meet above your head. Then return to the original position by jumping and lowering the arms in a return arch. Try to move lightly and smoothly and repeat for three sets of ten.

JUMPING ROPE

Jumping rope is an excellent exercise and it is used by many boxers because it builds endurance and coordination and timing. You can jump swinging the rope backwards or crosshanded to keep the movement from being repetitious.

Begin with two minutes per session and do three sets of two minutes at a time.

As well as helping the heart and lungs function more efficiently, jumping rope should help you move more quickly, lightly and surely on your feet as well as improving your coordination in general.

RUNNING IN PLACE

Running is a fairly quick and simple way of getting the heart pumping and the lungs working while building up the basic leg muscles. Instead of doing the minimum amount of effort, try to lift your knees high when running in place and let the leg action exercise the hips as well as the knees. Run for about three minutes and then walk around the room and then resume running for another three minutes. Pump your arms and be sure to relax the shoulders when you run. Do not hunch up the shoulders unconsciously. Experiment with the exercises and see what they do. It isn't necessary to do all three of these basic forms if you prefer doing one for a longer period of time. Of the three, jumping rope is the more complex, complete and beneficial to your health.

Stretching Exercises

Always do stretching slowly and gradually in a progressive way. Be prepared to allow time to produce improvement over a period of months. If you injure yourself in training you've done something wrong through carelessness or impatience.

If you hold the following exercises in the extreme position of tension, you are also cultivating power. In this way, the exercises can combine stretching with isometrics which also builds flexibility and power. Both are important elements for your own health and well-being and for executing the self-defense techniques well.

Allow time to stretch and strengthen the muscles required. Try to relax the leg while it is in motion and allow the momentum to help it move. Avoid jerky, sudden movements in all your exercises.

FRONT STRETCH

This exercise stretches the long muscles that run along the top or front of the thighs. It also helps develop muscles at the lower portion of the back that are vital for good body tone and health. It is beneficial for general strength in kicking techniques and flexibility of the upper leg.

Place one foot a long step in front of the other and sink into a deep stance. There should be slight channel between your feet for balance and the leg extended to the rear should be stretched out fully. Place both hands on the forward thigh and make sure that the spine is erect. Let the extended leg stretch fully and hold the position.

Now turn the upper body to one side, rotating the spine by turning the shoulders as much as possible. Place the hand behind the back for added tension and look back at the rear foot. Hold this position and allow the muscles to stretch.

THE BASIC LEG STRETCH

This exercise stretches the long muscles in the leg, particularly those running the length of the back of the leg. It also stretches the back and lower back muscles. It will help you develop general flexibility in the legs that can even be felt in walking. This is essential for good kicking techniques.

Start by placing one leg on a firm support that is at least waist high, such as a chair. You can use a table, wet bar, cabinet, or any other household furniture. Lean forward slowly and reach out with both hands grasping the foot. Allow your body to rest on your leg and your forehead to rest on your knee. Try to relax completely to help you reach full extension. This exercise does not require repetition so much as time to loosen the muscles that are being stretched. You may feel feedback at first, but allow several minutes of tension to prompt the muscles to extend.

Repeat the exercise with the other leg in the same way. Gradual practice over a period of time will make this exercise easier for you to do. If you are tense or the legs seem stiff, you can massage the muscles at the back of the thing or calf with one hand to warm and loosen them up. Do not bounce into this position but allow time for the muscles to become supple.

CIRCULAR KICK

This is a more advanced exercise, particularly good for people with some training in the martial arts. Beginners should work on it gradually in a progressive way. It develops flexibility of the groin muscles and inner thigh, as well as the muscles that lift and extend the legs. It will also develop muscles in the lower back area. The general benefits are overall flexibility of the legs and it is particularly helpful for martial arts kicking techniques.

Grasp a chair as a point of balance standing slightly behind it. Swing one leg up from the ground in a loop, as high as you can, moving clockwise (forward) and up. As your leg reaches maximum height, allow your torso to move forward and down to the back of the chair still maintaining your grip on the chair back. The leg continues backward in a loop, fully extended at all times. The exercise finishes as the leg returns to its original position and the torso returns to an upright posture.

Repeat the circular kick ten times on each side, trying to make your movement smooth and fluid.

FRONT CIRCULAR KICK

This exercise develops power in the leg muscles and flexibility both in leg and groin areas since it calls for full movement of the entire leg. It should be practiced gradually by beginners but it is an ideal exercise for persons already training in the martial arts. It also helps to build a sense of balance while in motion.

Take a forward stance with one leg, holding the upper body straight and relaxed. The hands are held loosely at the sides and the general body weight is slightly forward on the front foot. Step off the rear foot and start to bring the leg forward and up, moving across the front of the body slightly.

The leg is swung forward, slightly in and up in an arch while the opposite hand (in this case the left leg and right hand) is brought up and forward to slightly above the shoulder height. The leg continues upward in an arch to meet and brush across the outstretched hand at which point it is fully extended. The left hand is held back for balance.

The kicking leg now sweeps back in a circular arch to the outside and completes the loop by returning to the original starting point of the movement.

Beginners can attempt five repetitions and then repeat the movement with the opposite leg. Advanced or limber people can do ten repetitions of this kick. Although the movement is simple in its form, it requires flexibility and power. It should be done after several other preliminary leg stretches for best results.

BASIC STANDING CIRCULAR KICK

This exercise also develops the muscles that lift and kick as well as the inner thigh and groin muscles that are made more flexible. It helps to build balance and control in movement. It could be used as a basis for a high kick in some martial arts styles but here it is recommended as a general conditioner.

Take a chair and stand approximately two and a half feet behind it, facing its back.

Sweep the leg up in a kick moving from the inside to the outside, trying to make a complete circle in a counter clockwise direction. Eric has already reached about three quarters of the complete circle. The exercise is complete when the foot is back in its original position.

The chair will give you a target to work with for extension. As you progress, you will be able to move nearer to the chair. This kick should be done after limbering up with several of the static leg stretching exercises. Beginners can do five repetitions and then repeat the technique with the opposite leg. More advanced practitioners can do ten repetitions.

THE MODIFIED SPLIT

This exercise stretches the groin and inner thigh muscles, as well as the long muscles in the back of the legs. It provides overall flexibility that is useful in all leg techniques and builds general body tone.

Beginners and even practicing martial artists may want to use the chairs as a helpful tool in getting better results. Place two chairs facing each other with room between them for your body. Using the chairs as support for your arms, gradually lower yourself toward the floor, with legs outstretched to the front and rear. As the muscles stretch and lengthen, you can allow more weight to be brought upon them. Hold the position for a full minute. Then repeat on the opposite side and hold.

Advanced students can perform a front split without using the chair. Beginners can build to the point where the chairs are not needed after a period of time. Avoid moving suddenly or bouncing into the form to avoid any injury. If tension is felt in the legs, try to relax the muscles as much as possible. Beginners should allow a day of rest between strenuous warmup routines at first.

SIDE SPLIT STRETCH

This exercise stretches the groin and leg muscles, develops the lower back and the shoulders as well. It also helps build balance. It is useful for general toning and conditioning.

Take a wide stance and allow your legs to extend fully to each side just short of a complete side split. Bending forward at the waist, reach out with both arms to grasp your ankles.

Now extend the upper body forward and down so that the head almost touches the ground without letting go of the ankles. Return to the original position, repeat and hold in the lower position for maximum benefits. This exercise will develop control and strength in the entire body with demand put on the back and lower back as well as the arms and legs.

Advanced students can execute another variation on this exercise. In the lower position, release the ankles and put both hands forward on the ground in front of the shoulders, tighten the abdominal muscles, relax them, and then push up the upper body as though finishing a pushup. Repeat five times.

FLOOR STRETCH

This is a basic exercise that is common to many kinds of martial arts, yoga and exercise routines because it is so useful. It develops flexibility of the legs, back, shoulders and arms.

Sit on the floor with both legs stretched as far apart as possible. Keep the back and head erect. Without moving the position of the legs, reach forward and grasp one foot in both hands. Allow the upper body to rest on the outstretched leg. Let the head rest on the knee or shin, and make sure that both legs remain flat on the ground. Return to the original position, and repeat five times. Then repeat the same movement with the opposite leg. Repeat five times. Then allow the body to stretch completely forward, extending the arms directly ahead and rest on the ground. Then return to the upright position. Repeat this movement five times.

The exercise will be more effective if done in a slow and careful manner rather than in a hurried movement. An alternative to the repetitions and change in postures is to move from one side to the other and to the center and repeat the entire sequence again about five times. Hold each position for a count of thirty on the final repetition for maximum results.

REACHING STRETCH

This is a simple exercise but one that develops the lower back, flexibility in the arms and shoulders and helps promote balance.

Stand erect with feet spread slightly wider than your shoulders. Lower the upper body with the arms stretched directly forward until the upper body is perfectly horizontal. Now stretch forward as though straining to touch something that is just out of reach. Relax and raise body to an upright position and repeat. This time, hold the position and breathe slowly for one minute.

Follow up by doing the next exercise.

FORWARD BEND

From the reaching position of the previous exercise, continue to lower the upper body from the waist while bringing the arms around in an arch, past the legs and up behind the back. Push forward and down towards the front with your arms, and pull the torso toward your legs with the stomach muscles.

To test yourself, stand several feet from a wall and lower yourself into position trying to press the arms forward and touch the wall. When you have reached the limit, hold the position and breathe normally, for a count of thirty.

ARM SWINGS

The exercises done so far have worked on the legs and back with some emphasis on the stomach and shoulders. This exercise opens up the shoulder joint and is important for swings, punches and hand techniques of many kinds. Beyond the direct application, it is a basic exercise for toning and flexibility in the shoulders and also aids in reducing accumulated tension in this area.

Take a deep forward stance with the arms at the sides, hands in a fist. Swing both arms up in a circular motion, over the head, as far to the rear as possible and back to the original position, in a large smooth circle. Swing fully and smoothly for one minute.

Then swing the arms in a reverse arch from the back to the front, for one minute. Then change the stance to the opposite side and repeat the arm swing. As you loosen up the shoulder joints over a period of time, you can swing the arms in a fast circle. Loosen up gradually by swinging the arms at three-quarter speed from the beginning. Be sure to breathe normally and maintain a deep, solid stance.

BACK BEND

This exercise promotes flexibility of the spinal column which is a basis for general health and flexibility. If the spine is kept supple then the rest of the body will respond in a more flexible and total way.

Lie on the floor, draw the feet up and under the knees and reverse the arms next to the head, palms down. Push upwards slowly until the body forms a complete arch. Hold this position for one minute and then lower the body slowly to the floor.

For beginners who have difficulty in doing this exercise; have a partner hold the shoulders to support them and assist you to reach the back bend. After awhile you will be able to get into the position by yourself.

BUILDING POWER

There are several exercises which help build power through dynamic tension against resistance. These can be done with common objects or furniture found in your home.

Place a chair in front of you and take a deep forward stance as in the previous exercise. Place both hands on the back of the chair with the heels of the palms facing down on the chair top. Push downward with full force for a count of ten. Try to continue breathing normally. Repeat three times. You will gradually be able to exert force for longer periods of time.

TENNIS BALL SQUEEZE

To build strength in the grip and the arms as well all that you need is a tennis ball. Grasp it in one hand and squeeze as hard as possible for a ten count. Then repeat.

Shift the tennis ball to your other hand and repeat the exercise.

As a variation, grip the tennis ball, squeeze and release it forty times with one hand. Shift to the other hand and repeat squeezing and releasing it for another forty repetitions. The hands and forearms will develop more power as a result of continued practice.

LEG ISOMETRICS

This simple exercise will build power in your legs by isometrics; that is, by exerting force from one part of your body against an opposing part. The large thigh muscles that move the legs in kicking techniques will benefit most. General muscle tone will also be improved in the legs.

Sit erect on a straight chair, with your hands on your thighs. Bring your legs up to a horizontal position, straight in front of you. Loop one leg over the other at the ankle and lock the legs together. Now pull the legs apart trying to as hard as possible without actually releasing the locked position of the legs. The legs will both be developed by resisting against one another. Hold for a ten count, lock legs in the opposite direction and repeat. Advanced students should hold for a count of twenty.

STRETCHES WITH A PARTNER

Working out with a partner has the advantage of being able to get help in building flexibility. In the following two exercises, the partner can help you gain added suppleness in your legs by pushing you beyond your present limits. Work slowly and carefully and you will find that results will accumulate.

FRONT LEG STRETCH

Stand with your back against a wall for support and stretch your leg straight forward. Your partner can grasp your foot under the heel.

Your partner pushes slowly forward and up, stretching the muscles at the back of the leg and through the hip and pelvic area. Change sides and repeat the exercise, relaxing the leg as your partner stretches it. Hold the position at the peak for a ten count and then release. Move slowly and use common sense in finding your limit. Continue to work against your limit to increase your progress.

SIDE STRETCH

Stand sideways to the wall using your arm for support.

Extend your leg outward in a movement like a side kick and allow your partner to grasp it close to the ankle. Your partner can slowly raise your leg upward to stretch your groin and inner thigh muscles.

Hold the leg at its peak for a ten count and then lower it. Turn to the opposite side and repeat the exercise.

Both these exercises will help you develop greater flexibility throughout your legs particularly in the pelvic and groin areas. This will help you to execute the other kicking exercises more fully and enable you to do kicking techniques with greater power, speed and without fear of injury.

Summary

Regular practice is important. It is better to practice for a half hour or an hour a day four or five days a week than to practice for three hours just one day a week. Allow your body time to develop and respond to the exercises and you will be surprised at the results. There are many more exercises that could be done, but it is better to do a selected routine consistently than follow a hit-or-miss approach with a great many exercises.

Gradual progressive exercise will develop a flexible and healthy body that can do whatever you will demand of it. Beyond this, regular exercise is a good habit to have, particularly if you work in a sedentary job or spend much time during the day sitting at a desk. The benefits of being prepared to defend yourself include feeling more aware and confident and more in control of yourself and your own life.

CHAPTER SEVEN

Developing Mental Control

Mental Preparation And Training

If a trained fighter loses his self-control in an emergency it is just as though he or she had not trained at all. When you show fear, your give the advantage to the attacker. When you decide to fight, don't make a half-hearted attempt at it. Do not hold back. Make an attempt to dispose of the attacker quickly and completely. Fight all the way. Be meaner than your attacker. Fight like a vicious animal . . . but be mindful of your technique.

The element of surprise is your best weapon after all. Do the unexpected! Fake a move. Yell! Throw something to distract the assailant. Follow through with an attack to a vital spot. Run if you can. And always use your common sense . . . it might save your life.

To defend yourself successfully depends on your mental preparation as much as your physical preparation, perhaps more so. We often have more ability than we think we do, but it must be developed. There is no overnight success. What you put into it is what you get out; one minute invested in training is one minute out.

Mental preparation begins with concentration. Concentration is the ability to focus on one point, whether this is an idea, a technique or concentrating on something. Be calm and understand what it is that you are observing.

Concentration means to absorb more, to listen better, and to focus on a goal or a task more completely. This is the goal of this aspect of your practice.

People will often say, "How can I improve? I can't concentrate. . . ." or "I can't learn this, it is too complicated."

The answer is to begin with something simple and learn it completely and then move on to the next step. If you are already fairly good, you can still become better. As you begin the exercises that follow, allow yourself to be calm and relaxed. Let your mind and body slow down and put aside the other concerns and distractions that you may be involved with during the day. These techniques are simple but effective ways to begin utilizing your mental abilities more fully.

The use of self-defense requires that the individual have good reflexes, timing and speed. This is one way to develop good timing.

Concentration Exercises

THE TV SET DRILL

Facing the TV screen, plan a particular technique that you want to develop. Each time the scene changes on the screen, do the technique. What you are doing is reacting to an external stimulus without knowing when it is triggered . . . just as you would have to react in real life. Pick a TV show that is fast-paced with scene changes. It is better if you do it without the sound on so there is no clue as to when the picture shifts. Use one technique at first, then try a combination. Run through this drill for five minutes or so a day and in one month your timing will improve noticeably.

THE CANDLE TECHNIQUE

Light a candle in a dark room and place it about ten feet away. Sit looking at it quietly. The ancient Chinese use this to improve vision, concentration and meditation. The more calm you are, the better you are able to concentrate. If you are not concentrating on one point, your energy is scattered. You are trying to develop a calm mind, body and spirit. Do this exercise for ten minutes at a time.

THE OBSERVATION TECHNIQUE

Walk into a place that is new to you. Take one look all around you and then close your eyes and try to remember what you have seen. One good test is a store window. Try to remember all the objects displayed in the window. It could also be a schoolroom, a park, anywhere. You are attempting to build up your concentration and memory. If you keep it up; not only will your concentration improve, you will increase your awareness.

ONE THOUGHT

Sit quietly holding on to one particular thought and nothing else. If you think you cannot do it, it means that you cannot. Hold that thought for about three minutes.

TECHNIQUE DRILL

Sit down and mentally choose a technique that you wish to master. See yourself performing that technique. Visualize it fully as best you can. Perform it successfully. Your body will follow your mind.

It is also very important to be able to visualize yourself doing a technique fast . . . very fast. And visualize doing it with a lot of endurance. The mind will play a powerful part in your ultimate ability to actually do the technique. Train your mind as well as your body.

You must also learn to visualize yourself doing a fast combination and doing it (completely) with power. Some people approach learning a self-defense combination by trying to remember what comes next ... step by step but you should know the combination completely in its totality as one movement. If you begin to find that you can visualize yourself doing a combination fast and completely, then try to visualize different variations on it. This will make you mentally creative and also stimulate your thinking.

In approaching these exercises, try what seems comfortable to you. These exercises are presented here in a progressive way.

In approaching this book always think about improving today ... not on the past. Too many people think about their past, their disappointments and difficulties instead of thinking about ways to move forward and advance in their learning and their abilities. You might be surprised at how good you can be. Always maintain a positive and happy attitude.

I knew a woman who weighed over 200 pounds. She decided to practice martial arts and she made up her mind and went ahead and did it. She lost 100 pounds, became limber and became a very good martial artist. But this requires positive, not negative, concentration.

Awareness And Attitude

If you find yourself in a fight on the street and you lose, you must ask yourself why. Look into yourself and ask why did it happen in the first place. Was it your own problem that caused the situation to arise? Or were you in an actual situation of danger?

You may find yourself in a situation where you are looking at someone and you find him looking back. It is sort of an eye war. You tell yourself that he is looking for trouble. But when you start thinking like that, it shows immediately in your manner. If you start asking him what he is looking at, then you are beginning to get into a situation that could lead to trouble. *You*, yourself, are contributing to the problem by your attitude and actions. Somebody can get hurt or killed as a result of a needless eye war.

Another factor to remember is that even if you are good with fighting techniques, it doesn't mean that you can win every time. Many good tournament fighters are not very good on the streets. A street fighter may throw you off because he acts in a totally unorthodox way. I have seen a streetfighter put a national champion down with one shot.

Losing your common sense sometimes prompts you to take a chance that you shouldn't take. Your own life, and that of someone else, like your family, is more important than your ego or pride. In the case of a robbery, why risk your life for your possessions. If you have something really valuable, it should be insured or in a safe deposit box; then you don't have to worry or take a needless risk.

As a rule, the martial arts have always been related to the tradition of zen because it is essential not to get uptight but stay cool. We practice meditation to build up the ability to remain calm. This helps you to avoid overreacting to little things that constantly come up in life. When you get excited, the adrenaline starts to flow and then you get into trouble.

When you are upset, you should do something about it. Don't drive and don't go looking for trouble. Take a walk and calm down or call a good friend and talk it over. Punch a pillow instead of a person. What you want to avoid is losing your control. In some cases, you may end up needing to defend yourself because you have offended someone else. Instead, we should be learning how to live and act in a mature way. Stress and pressures help to lose your control so it is important to learn how to deal with stress whether that means seeing a therapist or getting more rest and relaxation.

Taking responsibility for your own life and your actions, as well as your self-defense skills, will help you deal with things without fear. You are less likely to be a victim and your attitude will be more positive towards life. Mental attitude is a part of your self-defense in a very important way. To illustrate this, we can say that the physical part of self-defense is a small slice of the total picture, common sense is a larger slice and general mental awareness and attitude is the biggest single slice of all.

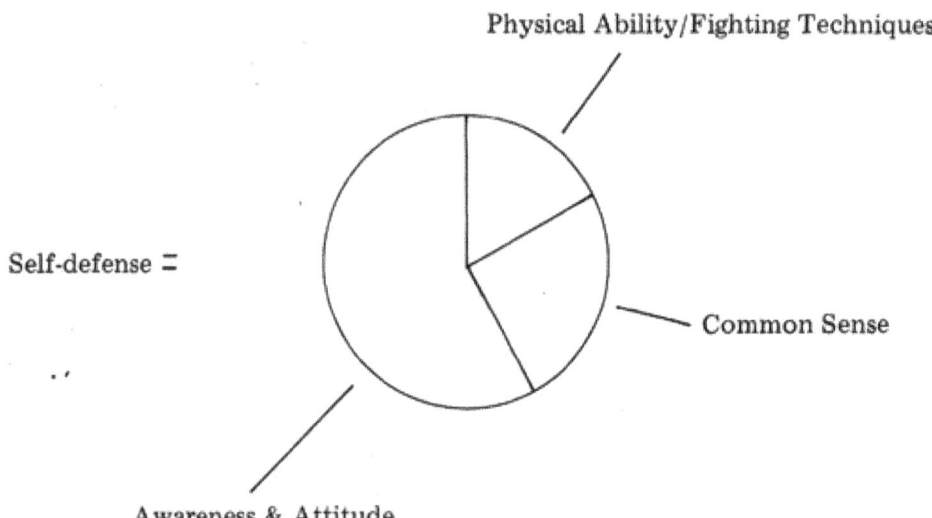

CHAPTER EIGHT

Summary

How to Choose A Self-Defense School

You should find out about several self-defense schools by asking your friends who are in the martial arts, checking the yellow pages and making inquiries. Visit at least three schools before even considering making a choice.

The point to remember is that you are interested in self-defense instruction primarily and not necessarily in a long term commitment to the martial arts as a hobby. Many schools emphasize philosophy, meditation, health and other benefits of this way of life which is very helpful to many people. But if your goal is to learn how to defend yourself in a relatively short period of time, you should question the instructor about his method of helping you do this. But do not ask him how quickly he can teach you since he may think you are overly impatient and insincere.

While you are at the school, try to evaluate the quality of the students—do you like the vibes, is it a place of respect and order? Be careful about signing long term contracts that will oblige you to pay if you wish to change your mind or stop training.

Talk to the instructor. He should be able to answer your questions clearly and give you his time. Don't let a sales pitch influence you. Be sure that you choose a place devoted to self-defense, rather than one with fancy equipment, saunas and comfort features. Instruction is what you are looking for. Make your choice carefully and you will find that you can learn a great deal. Improve your skills and health under the guidance of a good teacher.

Do's And Don'ts

Do practice with a partner.

Do warmup before practicing kicks and punches.

Do avoid making contact in practice strikes.

Do plan ahead when going somewhere new to you.

Do visualize yourself in danger and check your reactions.

Do practice on a regular basis.

Do practice simulating an attack.

Do understand how the techniques work.

Don't get into eye-wars on the street.

Don't get into arguments with strangers.

Don't wear provocative clothing.

Don't hitchhike.

Don't walk alone or unescorted at night.

Don't display money or jewelry obviously.

Don't practice with real knives or bottles.

Don't injure your practice partner.

Don't reveal plans to strangers on the telephone.

Don't invite strangers into your home.

General Review Quiz

1. In case of threatened rape, you should: 1) start talking 2) fight back immediately 3) call for help.
2. If you are threatened with a gun: 1) grab it away from the attacker 2) see what he wants and give it to him 3) reach for a handy weapon.
3. The best choice of kick for self-defense is: 1) to the chest 2) to the head 3) to the knee.
4. Facing an attacker, the best stance is: 1) turning your back 2) facing him directly 3) a forty-five degree angle sideways.
5. In facing a dangerous situation, first: 1) react quickly 2) remain calm 3) start fighting.
6. The best way to avoid purse snatching is: 1) give it to the robber 2) carry a weapon in the purse 3) don't carry a purse at all.
7. In getting into your car, the first thing to do is: 1) lock the doors 2) drive away quickly 3) turn on your lights.
8. Best way to avoid violence is: 1) carry a gun 2) take ten years of martial arts training 3) take preventive precautions.
9. If you need to call for help, the best method is: 1) cry "help" 2) yell "police" 3) yell "fire."
10. The most vulnerable points on the body are: 1) chest and stomach 2) forehead and elbow 3) eyes and groin.
11. For safety in the home you should: 1) always leave lights on 2) have emergency numbers taped on the phone 3) put a black belt on your door.
12. To stop obscene phone calls: 1) reason with the caller 2) don't answer the phone at night 3) have an unlisted phone number.
13. Seeing a suspicious person in your elevator, you should: 1) keep an eye on him in the elevator 2) tell him you're a karate champ 3) take the next elevator.
14. When a delivery man arrives at your home, you should: 1) invite him in and check his ID 2) have him wait outside 3) go outside to pick up the package.
15. In self-defense, the best method is: 1) a surprise strike 2) jumping away from danger 3) wrestle the attacker to the ground.
16. Waiting for a bus, train or subway, you should: 1) have a gun concealed 2) stand in a well-lit area 3) check the schedules so you don't have to wait long.

17. Your best offensive physical weapons are: 1) butting the attacker with your head 2) grabbing the attacker's arm 3) a knee kick to the groin.
18. Home burglary precautions that protect you best are: 1) a sign on the door for alarm system 2) stay at home evenings 3) install protective equipment.
19. It is not always best to rely on weapons to protect yourself because: 1) they can be used against you 2) you may lose the weapon 3) you might injure yourself using it.
20. Walking alone at night, try to: 1) walk in the middle of the street 2) walk on the dark side 3) walk on the opposite side from the dark side.
21. Self-defense works best when you: 1) hit someone else first 2) get friends to help you 3) use it only when threatened.
22. If you approach a vicious dog, try to: 1) scare him by noises 2) take another route 3) find a weapon to hold.
23. Using tear gas or mace is legal: 1) always 2) after dark 3) when you are licensed to.
24. In exercising, the best way to begin is: 1) fast, bouncy stretches 2) no stretching 3) slow, gradual warmups.
25. When defending yourself, you should always: 1) knock out the attacker 2) try not to hurt the attacker much 3) do what you must to prevent injury to yourself.

Review Quiz Answers

1. Start talking.
2. See what he wants and give it to him.
3. To the knee.
4. Forty-five degree angle sideways.
5. Remain calm.
6. Don't carry a purse.
7. Lock the doors.
8. Take preventive precautions.
9. Yell "fire."
10. Eyes and groin.
11. Have emergency numbers on your phone.
12. Have an unlisted number.
13. Take the next elevator.
14. Have him wait outside.
15. Surprise strike.
16. Check the schedules so you don't wait unnecessarily long.
17. A knee to the groin.
18. Install equipment.
19. They can be used against you.
20. Walk on the lighter side.
21. Use it only when threatened.
22. Take another route.
23. When you are licensed.
24. Slow, gradual warmup.
25. Do what you must to prevent injury to yourself.

Conclusions

This book has presented a selection of techniques to protect you from attack situations on the street, some measures to prevent you becoming a victim of violence, and some ideas to help you deal with violence in daily life with confidence based on real ability and skill.

Each section can be studied and referred to over a period of time until you absorb the ideas and principles contained within. Practicing and using the drills, exercises and techniques will bring the material to life and make it a part of your own way of handling emergencies as well as your own daily life.

Eric Lee: King Of Kata

Hollywood is a long way from Eric's family business, a Chinese restaurant, in Oakland, California. Although he was more or less expected to take on his share of the operation, Eric had other plans in mind. First, to study the martial arts, and then later, to pursue his interest in acting. Eric and his family came to the United States in 1962. They had lived for several years in Hong Kong after leaving his birthplace in the Chung Shan Village of Canton Province, China.

Like many other people in the martial arts, Eric Lee began his training because he was small. He wanted the mental confidence and physical protection that skill in the martial arts provides, but like others, he soon realized that there were many other benefits and advantages to this kind of training. Now he hopes to share some of what he has learned with others, in the hopes that they will find more security and peace of mind in a world afflicted with needless violence.

Eric's knowledge of self-defense techniques and principles comes from a wide background. He combines extensive experience in a number of martial arts styles and traditions with a no nonsense approach to self-defense. He also stresses the correct mental attitude in learning and applying the techniques, without which, physical ability can be useless. Eric likes to say that, "If you see yourself as small, you cannot accomplish big things. If you see yourself as a success, you'll probably be one."

Eric has demonstrated that positive attitudes lead to genuine achievement through his own career in the martial arts world. He has achieved great heights in both non-contact fighting tournaments and forms demonstrations as well. For a decade or more, he has been known throughout the martial arts world as the "King of Kata."

Kata is the Japanese word for the sets of continuous movements used to practice the various fighting techniques while developing speed, concentration and stamina. To execute kata correctly requires the physical and mental control of a professional athlete with the aesthetic and dramatic sense of a competitive gymnast or dancer.

Eric raised the format of tournament kata to a new level of excitement and skill. In recognition of his mastery of this form, he was named United States champion in 1972 and 1973. During this period he won over seventy first place titles as well as two Golden Fist Awards for Outstanding Kung Fu Kata and Outstanding Chinese Weapons Stylist.

From this point on, Eric toured with the Oriental Expo, the Masters of the Martial Arts Expo and the World Martial Arts Expo. It was a natural expansion of his career to get into movie stunt work where he could perform dramatic fight sequences and begin his hand at acting.

Getting small parts in action films, Eric began learning his new craft by studying with several noted drama coaches in Hollywood. He soon landed parts in films such as THE KILLER ELITE, THE DEATH MACHINE and GOOD GUYS WEAR BLACK. He has chalked up a starring role in the FALCON'S CLAW and a lead part in THE SHINOBI. His most recent screen credit, however, is the starring role in a major action film, WEAPONS OF DEATH.

Eric's martial art training began in 1966 under See Chung Ball, who taught a traditional kung fu style. Eric went on to study a variety of styles, including Won Hop Kuen Do, and then he began training with a number of martial artists in the Oakland, California area. Among them was Al Dascascos, who specializes in kajukembo. Eric also practiced with many black belts from various fighting methods as he continued in his development.

Eric went on to demonstrate his range of abilities in the martial arts as well as a positive attitude toward whatever goals he sets and whatever projects he undertakes. This is one of the valuable lessons he hopes to pass on to others as a teacher and performer.

ERIC LEE:
THE KING OF FORMS

As a competitor, he set an example for all martial artists to follow. His dynamic and powerful performances in the kata and sparring divisions made Eric Lee one of the top competitors ever and one of the all-time sought after instructors around the world. With an incredible physique and remarkable technical skills, Lee amazed not only students but also well-known instructors of different martial arts style who came to him to improve their forms for competition. Although strongly rooted in tradition, he represented the eclectic approach to the martial arts. In his mind, the search for knowledge was more important than an allegiance to any established system or method. His philosophy of life was based on balanced and "happy thinking," as he liked to say. Even though he was very modern in his approach to martial arts, he displayed all the true spiritual qualities of a well-trained and well-versed traditional kung-fu man. He was a true ambassador of the ancient Shaolin Temple who walked the roads of the 21st century.

How long have you been practicing martial arts?

For over forty years now. The first few years I wasn't that serious about my training, it was simply for fun. I become serious when I got beaten-up by some bullies. They had fun pushing people around and one day it was my turn. It was a very bad experience because I stayed laying in the field almost choking! I practiced different methods of fighting but I don't believe in one style. Every style is a personal view of several different principles. Mainly I have trained in Northern Shaolin, kajukenbo, wun hup kuen do, wing chun and tai chi. I'm not proficient in all the styles I practiced, but I studied them and learned a great deal.

Many years ago I was living in Oakland where Bruce Lee had his school. I trained under James Y. Lee in the '60s. At that time the method Sifu James Lee was teaching was called Jun Fan Gung-Fu. Sifu James Lee was very direct. He didn't hold to any tradition and he wanted to be effective above everything else. The techniques at that time were very simple, pak sao, lop sao and straight blast with a few kicks added. I wish I had the opportunity to train under Bruce Lee because he was an innovator and a pioneer in many ways, not only physically but also philosophical as well. My teachers also were Al Dacascos in wun hop kuen do and sifu Ken Chong in wing chun gung fu. I trained in chi kung with Share K. Lew in San Diego , medical chi kung with Dr. Hua Huang and I'm currently training qi qong under Wen Mei Ju, who I consider one of the top instructors in the world in this method of Chinese martial arts. During one of my visits to Hong Kong, I studied tai chi and hung gar kuen, the style of the tiger and crane. This system is a very powerful kung-fu style and it is interesting that I am re-assessing the practice of some of the traditional forms. It amazing how you body uses the energy a different way when you get older. At this moment, I'm really interested in learning about the healing arts, and surprisingly, due to muscle memory, your body opens the meridians that you used many years ago in training the forms – the techniques feel different. I also training in AG Matrix System with grandmaster and founder Mr. Al Garza.

My father is a herbalist in Hong Kong and I learned a lot about how to use the herbs to improve your physical health and to recover your body after intensive training sessions. This knowledge helped me a lot in my martial arts career.

I enjoy learning movements that I can adapt and modify when you reach a high level in the martial arts. You need to know different methods so you can face different opponents and situations. For instance, if you face a judo man, you don't want to grapple with him because he is going to defeat you easily. Then you need to have another method that you can use to balance the situation. The old one-system approach is not good enough these days. You need to look and learn different techniques so you can use those that are appropriate a particular moment. I'm fascinated by knowledge and not by styles.

Did you have any memorable experiences when you were competing?

When I was competing I had great time. I was one of the top competitors back then. I remember I had a friend who was a magician. I was teaching him kung-fu and he was teaching me magic. It was a good trade and fun also. But I'd love to tell one story that still is very much alive in my mind. Due to my obsession with kung-fu it, many nights I couldn't go to sleep and relax. One day I learned a double-sword form so I went to the park very early in the morning to practice. Then a little baby bird fell from a tree. I picked him up and suddenly dozens of birds appeared from nowhere and started to attack me. It was like the Alfred Hitchcock movie "The Birds." I was so scared that I began to use the swords to defend myself. In fact, I chopped a few birds! They poked at me and I ended up bleeding. I put the bird in the shirt pocket and ran to my car. The birds chased me all the way to the car and once there I couldn't find the key. Then, I put the bird down to look for the key in my pockets and most of the birds stopped attacking me. I finally made it inside the car and to my surprise some of them got into the car with me! Finally, I got rid of them. It was crazy. I promised never to pick up a bird again. Now If I want to have a bird, I go and buy one!

Is it true you were inspired by old kung-fu movies?

Yes, it is. The old movies display a lot of the great traditional values found in the Chinese martial arts. Kwon Duk Hing was an actor in the old kung-fu movies from China and he strongly impressed me. He always played the part of the great hung gar master Wong Fei Hung. They were black and white movies and they inspired me very much – you know all the traditional stories and adventures. In fact, when I started to compete, other competitors used make fun of me because I was wearing the traditional kung-fu uniform. I remember a lot of things these characters did in the movies and I decided to compete in the sparring division to prove I could fight too. Later, I ended up taking home trophies for both kata and sparring!

Has your personal expression of the art changed over the years?

My father was very influential in my training. When I was very young I went to Hong Kong to live. Everything in my early training was very traditional – very formal. I spent time in the Chinese Opera and this really made an impact on me. Today, I'm not that traditional as far as the techniques go, but I'm traditional in the moral and ethical aspects of the art. You need the traditional way to develop a good foundation, but after years of traditional training you can expand your horizons and taste different arts. This is called "cross-training" today. I enjoy looking at several arts and absorbing different methods. Even if you are on a diet, you still can read the menu. All these elements have definitely changed the way I express kung-fu.

I believe that having an open mind is extremely important. Fortunately, teachers have an open mind for students too, otherwise we couldn't have as many kung-fu schools as we have today. Don't forget that in the old times, the sifu hardly accepted any students. They were very interested in your character first, not your money, and this made the schools packed with students as we can see today.

Were you a natural, or did you work hard to get to a good technical level?

I don't think I was very natural. I had to train really hard for competition and to improve my technique. The science of training those days wasn't as advanced as today. We basically stayed in the school all the time and repeated the movements over and over. I remember that we used music to spice our training, but it wasn't like what we know today as tae bo. We used the music to develop the necessary rhythm for kata competition. At this moment health is my priority. The arts gave me a lot of things. I'm a successful person. Sometime people think of success in terms of monetary rewards, but there are many other ways of being successful in martial arts – you meet great people and you have the opportunity to travel around the world and meet other masters and learn from them as well. All these things – when you are no longer interested in competing – are truly priceless. These are the things that stay with you forever.

How is the Western kung-fu level compared to the technical level in China?

Don't forget that for many years kung-fu was prohibited in China. In America, when people take something and break it down and re-structure it, they create a new format. I'm a product of an American mentality, I'm an eclectic martial artist. I don't have any limitations or boundaries that prevent me from absorbing knowledge from different sources. In China, this wouldn't be possible because the environment is more traditional. A good instructor, regardless of being Caucasian or Chinese, should have patience with the students. Patience is the most important aspect; this is followed by setting and teaching by example. A teacher should be physically fit because he is the example for his students. I remember that in the beginning of my teaching days I was expecting my students to perform the techniques perfectly right away, but they didn't. I learned that different students learn and absorb the material at different speeds. You, as their instructor, must be sensitive to that and help them to improve accordingly. Kindness and patience are the keys.

Do you consider yourself a traditionalist or a modernist?

For many years I tried to develop a system with explosive techniques; but as I got older I found out that you have to strive to be deceptive and capable of flowing with your opponent's movements. It's not about what you want to do but how you react to what is given to you by your aggressor. To some extent, I consider myself a modernist because I truly believe in the approach that allows the student to incorporate principles and techniques from different systems. I don't think students should be limited by any external boundaries that prevent them from achieving their potential as martial artists and human beings. I like to experiment and exchange ideas, concepts and strategies with other martial artists because it helps me to improve and to express myself through the arts. On other hand, I feel that I am a very traditional martial artist because I strongly advocate for the traditional values of martial arts like respect, humility, and honor.

What can you tell us about the self-defense aspects of kung-fu?

Self-defense is a very tricky aspect of the martial arts. For me, self-defense falls in a whole different category because it involves a series of external factors that are not present in the average martial arts school. You may be a great kicker, forms performer, and very skillful in all the techniques – but not be able to teach self-defense. You can win many tournaments and be great in sparing and it won't mean anything in a street fight. I would advise to those interested in self-defense to research and find the right school for this purpose. There are five basic elements necessary to build a good self-defense system: simplicity – complex or elaborate techniques can easily fail through lack of proper execution; surprise – try to catch your assailant unaware; speed – move fast and with determination; impact – work to develop power; follow-up – don't stop after the first hit – keep hitting until you are completely out of the situation.

How does diet and nutrition affect martial arts?

Diet is an important part of your life, because your body operates with what you put in it. Without the proper nutrients in the body, you simply cannot perform your best. It's that simple. It's like being a machine that doesn't have the necessary fuel to run or the raw material to repair itself. I eat a lot of fresh fruits and vegetables, stay away from sugar and greasy foods, and have a good sources of protein. It is advisable to supplement that with vitamins, minerals and Chinese herbs. They will improve your energy levels if you work and train hard. My basic advice is to keep your nutrition clean and simple, covering all the basic elements. The right foods and proper exercises will bring health to you.

Do you recommend a specific personal training program?

It is hard for me to recommend a specific training program because I have changed mine so many times. It all depends where you are going and what your goals are. There are some general principles you should always include, though. Endurance training with exercises such as running; isometric exercises for power and strength; explosive drills with or without a partner, using bag work and focus mitts; and stretching using both dynamic and static stretching exercises. Don't forget to include sensitivity drills, such as sticky hands training. The mental aspects should be cultivated through meditation and visualization training. As far as weight training, I recommend using light weights and high number of repetitions with a slow steady pace, then add a quick burst. This simple technique will help you to develop the capacity for sudden, explosive power. If you put all these elements in your training routine, you'll have a complete package. Vary your training schedule every once in a while to focus on different aspects of the whole picture.

How do you approach physical training in the martial arts?

From the very beginning, my approach to competition was to make it part of my life, without upsetting the natural processes of my day-to-day existence. Diet, physical training, mental discipline and recreation – all these elements of life are equally important factors in the presentation of forms. There is absolutely no way I could have been successful without attending to each of these elements individually, every day. The music, the lights and the dramatic presentations were merely part of a whole. It is very important to understand that training is a whole process. The entire body and mind must benefit from that process. Now, I don't pretend to be able to tell other people what sort of conditioning program they should abide by, but for me the practice has to begin with diet. For being in shape for competition, training hard is about 50 percent of the job and nutrition is the other 50 percent. You can't perform at your best, no matter how much you train for an event, if your body lacks essential nutrients. Also if you train hard every day – do a lot of running and so on – but your body doesn't have the right nutrients, then you are just using your body up.

Do you like to run?

It's better to run every other day than to make a religious daily regimen out of it. The body needs a certain amount of time to recuperate. Sure you can run more than that, but it gets to be a case of diminishing returns. Besides, there are other things to do in training that work on the aerobic system. I like to combine running with a program of isometrics and limited weight training. I lift weights on a very light schedule two or three times a week, working on specific muscle groups that are important in martial arts techniques. The idea is not to build too much muscle tissue, which doesn't really help in performing forms, but to build strength. I lift the weight very slowly most of the way through its arc, and then speed-up suddenly, concentrating on strengthening the ligaments.

You were known in your competition days for having extremely deep concentration when performing. How did you reach that level of concentration?

In exercise, concentration is most important. I can spend 15 minutes working on a particular exercise, and if I'm concentrating well I can get more out of that than I would in two hours otherwise. I use the same pattern of exertion in doing calisthenics as I do in weight training – slow, steady effort, then a quick burst. This helps to develop the capacity for sudden, explosive energy, which is a crucial aspect of martial arts technique. It's important to do the right kind of exercises and do them in the way that is most rewarding and applicable to the purpose you have in mind.

Can you give an example?

In upper-body work, when I'm doing push-ups, rather than trying to do as many as I possibly can, I prefer to do several rapid sets of 25, and rest for a minute or two between sets. Again, that helps develop the kind of explosive power I want. Then from there I'll pump a few weights and then go into some isometrics. Exercise cannot be seen as a purely physical activity. To gain the greatest good from it you also have to work on concentration and breathing. I breathe steadily during isometric exercises, never letting the air build up or the blood rush to my head. In other forms of exercise, I usually breathe out with the exertion and in with the return. Breathing correctly is crucial for the health of both heart and lungs, and should always be calm, regular and unhurried. This may seem a little difficult at first, but it pays off and becomes second nature after awhile. By the same token, the mind should always be clam and unstressed, no matter what the body is doing. When I am training, all the stress is on my muscles and my mind remains clam. This is how to gain the maximum from training.

How has the tournament circuit developed over the years?

When I first started, judges weren't looking for showmanship in forms competition. Traditionally, they looked for speed and power – for how effective the form seemed – but not for how flashy or difficult the techniques were or how much showmanship the performer could generate. Of course, the forms were not originally designed for competition or entertainment, but strictly to develop certain techniques. In the first tournaments I participated in, musical forms were not even permitted. We were the first ones who included music in demonstrations, and from there it gradually filtered into competition as well – there was a music division in many tournaments only for the last few years of my competitive career. But what happened was that martial arts movies started coming out and monopolizing the showmanship element of the martial arts. People in the movies were starting to display more showmanship than people in live demonstrations. Today, there are still a lot of tournaments that try to exclude the more theatrical aspects of forms from competition, but at least nowadays people in a live demonstration can be compared favorably to what's being done in film. Personally, I didn't add the music as a nice little touch for the audience. I usually train with music, too. For one thing, it makes training more fun, just as it makes the performance more entertaining for the audience.

There is nothing wrong with having a good time in martial arts. But the musical rhythm also helped me to develop my own internal cadence for the form. As you follow the music, you'll get a feel for the rhythm of your own performance, and that adds to your creative impulses and spontaneity. Training to music should be a total creative experience. This is not something that is easy to achieve, especially not on the strength of just listening to a song one. But if you listen to the music 20 times or so, and really begin to get to know it, you can reach a new plateau of creativity. You get to where you can vary your movement rhythm any time you want. Naturally, you shouldn't rely on music, but it can be a significant part of forms training. In forms competition today, the tempo, the rhythm and the performance are becoming ever more significant and the people are getting better at it all the time.

Where are your current goals?

I try to live my live to my fullest. Sometimes you run into people who bring negative energy into your life and you have to keep them away from you. You might say that I'm addicted to working out and I need the martial arts in my life to be happy. My goal is to develop myself more in the internal arts, to become more knowledgeable about the internal aspects of kung-fu. Probably this is a natural progression due to my age. Now I know how to build energy from inside, and I have learned to use it in a more efficient way than when I was younger. Look at nature and you'll find the right way of doing things in your own life. Try to find a balance in life. Go out with friends and have a social life too. Some people only want to be by themselves in an isolated environment and spend all their free time training in martial arts. This is not good – you have to bring balance to your life by relating to other human beings and enjoying other things in life that are not martial arts related. Then you really will succeed in kung-fu – because kung-fu is, after all, simply a matter of proper balance in life.

What direction do you see martial arts going in the future?

I think people will go more and more into the cross-training approach I mentioned before. What they have to understand is that in order to become good in this approach, you must spend time with a good teacher to build a foundation. Don't jump from one style to another without a good foundation. After you have that strong base, give always credit to your teachers and move on to other styles that you feel may bring something good to you. Remain open and enjoy your friends and your life because that's also part of a good kung-fu practitioner. And don't forget to think happy.

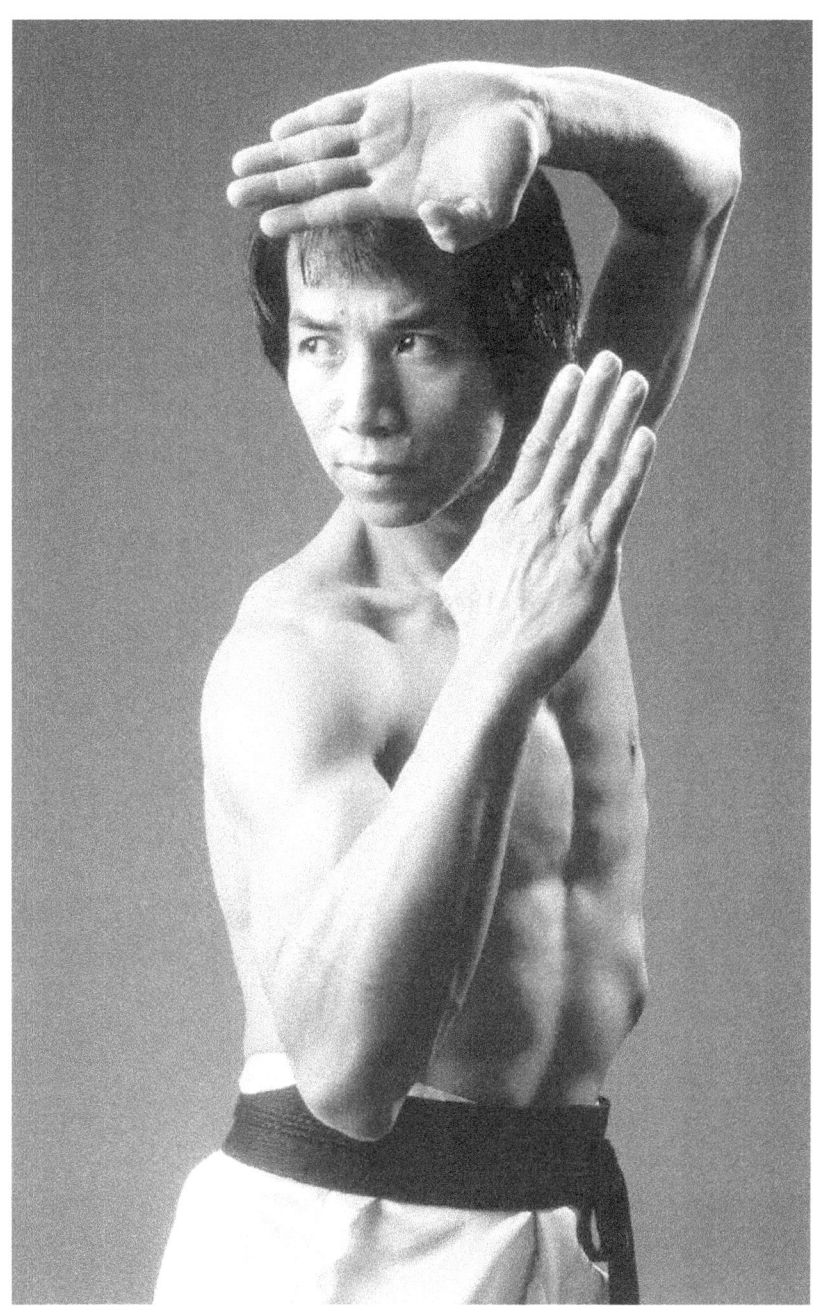